CLASSIC AMERICAN WRITERS

HERMAN MELVILLE

REBECCA STEFOFF

JULIAN ⓜ MESSNER
Published by Simon & Schuster
New York   London   Toronto   Sydney   Tokyo   Singapore

Photo Acknowledgments:
Cover and Title Page: Courtesy of the Berkshire Athenaeum, Pittsfield, Mass.
Title Page: Herman Melville in 1861, a decade after *Moby-Dick* was published.
Page iv: New York Public Library Picture Collection.
Page 6: Courtesy of the Berkshire Athenaeum, Pittsfield, Mass.
Page 14: Courtesy of the Berkshire Athenaeum, Pittsfield, Mass.
Page 18: Bettmann/Hulton.
Page 31: New York Public Library Picture Collection.
Page 34: Courtesy of the Peabody & Essex Museum, Salem, Mass.
Page 46: Bettmann/Hulton.
Page 63: Courtesy of the Berkshire Athenaeum, Pittsfield, Mass.
Page 67: New York Public Library Picture Collection.
Page 83: The Bettmann Archive.
Page 88: Courtesy of the Berkshire Athenaeum, Pittsfield, Mass.
Page 93: The Bettmann Archive.
Page 108: Courtesy of the Berkshire Athenaeum, Pittsfield, Mass.
Page 121: The Bettmann Archive.
Page 131: New York Public Library Picture Collection.

JULIAN MESSNER
Published by Simon & Schuster
1230 Avenue of the Americas, New York, New York 10020
Copyright © 1994 by Rebecca Stefoff

Book design by Virginia Pope
JULIAN MESSNER and colophon are trademarks of Simon & Schuster

Manufactured in the United States of America

10 9 8 7 6 5 4 3 2 1
Library of Congress Cataloging-in-Publication Data
Stefoff, Rebecca.
    Herman Melville / by Rebecca Stefoff.
        p.   cm. — (Classic American writers)
    Includes bibliographical references (p.) and index.
    1. Melville, Herman, 1819–1891—Juvenile literature.   2. Novelists,
American—19th century—Biography—Juvenile literature.   [1. Melville,
Herman, 1819–1891.   2. Authors, American.]   I. Title. II. Series.
PS2386.S74 1994   813' .3—dc20   [B]   93-11751   CIP   AC
                        ISBN 0-671-86771-7

CONTENTS

*Nuku Hiva's rugged landscape is a legacy of its volcanic origin.
The island's sheer cliffs and cloud-wrapped peaks turned the escape of Melville
and Toby into an ordeal.*

GRIM BEGINNINGS

In July of 1842, three ships lay at anchor in a bay on the coast of Nuku Hiva, a tiny island in the south Pacific Ocean. Two of the ships were French, for the Marquesas Islands, of which Nuku Hiva was the largest, had just come under French control, and the French navy and merchant fleet had begun stopping at the island to take on water and food. The third vessel was the *Acushnet*, an American whaling ship. From its deck a young seaman named Herman Melville anxiously scanned the shore.

He saw a Polynesian paradise. Nuku Hiva was lush with tropical vegetation, swaying palm trees, and twining vines. The island rose steep and green from a clear blue sea. A narrow sandy beach rimmed the shore where a valley opened onto the sea from the mountainous interior of the island. Marquesan islanders, graceful and strong, glided across the bay in canoes or swam out to visit the ships.

Nuku Hiva was a splendid, exotic scene. It must have appeared glorious—almost unearthly—to Melville, who had spent most of his twenty-two years in rugged New York State.

On that July day, as Melville studied the shore, he was not admiring the landscape, however. He was planning an escape route.

Melville and a shipmate named Toby had decided to desert the *Acushnet*. They had made their plans carefully, in secret. By the law of the sea, desertion was a serious offense. If the captain or one of the ship's mates had suspected their intentions, the two men would probably have been imprisoned to prevent their escape.

Toby and Melville gathered what supplies they could hide under their clothes: a little food, a few personal belongings, and as much tobacco as they could get, both to smoke and to trade with the islanders for food. Then, when they learned that the *Acushnet* was almost ready to raise anchor and depart, they managed to go ashore with one of the last shore parties. The two men, seizing their opportunity, slipped away from their companions during a thundershower, dashed into the forest, and made their way to a ridge at the end of the beach. They hoped to reach the safety of a valley on the other side of the mountains.

After clambering to the top of the ridge and climbing a rugged cliff, Toby and Melville reached the top of one of Nuku Hiva's mountains a few hours before sunset. To their dismay, they did not see the broad, welcoming valley they had expected to find. Instead, they looked out across a wilderness of rough, uninhabited country. They had hoped to find coconuts and fruit growing everywhere in the mountains, not realizing that in Nuku Hiva food plants were cultivated and grew only near villages. Now they were alarmed to realize that they would get no new provisions until they reached a friendly village. To make matters worse, Melville had injured a leg in his dash away from the *Acushnet*.

The deserters spent the night in the open. On the following morning they pushed on across the knife-edged peaks. Finally, in the afternoon, they found themselves looking down into a valley. But *which* valley? From listening to sailors and islanders in the bay, Melville had learned that two tribes lived in two different valleys in the mountains of Nuku Hiva. One tribe, the Happas, had been described as hospitable and peaceful. However, the other tribe, the Taipis, were regarded with fear and dread, for they were said to be cannibals. The greatest fear Melville and Toby had was falling into their hands. Now, as they stood gazing down at the huts and farm plots on the distant valley floor, they wondered whether they dared risk descending. What if this were the Taipi valley? Would they be walking into certain death?

Toby thought they should take the chance. The valley offered food, and they were beginning to be desperately hungry. But Melville insisted that they cross another ridge and try to make their way into a smaller, more remote valley, where they might be able to find food without running into hostile Marquesans. Unfortunately, Melville had a hard time following his own plan—climbing up toward the ridge was exceedingly painful because of his injured leg. That night, he and Toby slept in the open again, damp and discouraged.

The next morning, after surveying the distant ridge, Melville knew that he could not make the climb. He agreed to follow Toby's suggestion. He only hoped that their descent into the first valley they had seen would not bring them to a gruesome fate.

Herman Melville was thousands of miles from his family, a deserter from his ship, with no sure way of getting home again. He was hurt, hungry, and heading toward a village that he feared might be violently unfriendly. As he rose wearily to his feet to begin the climb down into the valley, Herman Melville was a young man with a very uncertain future.

Herman Melville was no stranger to uncertainty. His family had known grief and poverty, and he had grown to maturity in an atmosphere of worry, restlessness, and stress.

Melville was always proud of his family background—especially of the fact that both his grandfathers had fought for American independence in the Revolutionary War. One grandfather, General Peter Gansevoort, was of Dutch ancestry. General Gansevoort became a hero during the American Revolution by defending Fort Stanwix in northern New York from British and Native American attackers. After the war, Gansevoort settled in Albany and was regarded as one of the richest men in the area. Gansevoort's daughter Maria was Herman Melville's mother.

The Melville side of the family was distantly related to an aristocratic family in Scotland. Herman's paternal grandfather, Major Thomas Melville, also played a prominent role in the American fight for independence. He was among the Bostonians who dressed as Indians and dumped British tea into the harbor in the well-known Boston Tea Party, a protest against taxes that helped start the Revolutionary War. As a boy visiting his grandparents' home, Herman was awed by the sight of a small bottle on the mantlepiece above the Melville fireplace. It contained tea leaves shaken from his grandfather's clothes after that historic occasion.

Major Melville's son Allan, who married Maria Gansevoort, went into business in New York City, importing and selling luxury goods such as silks and fine hats and gloves, mostly from France. Both he and Maria felt that it was important to show their prosperity to the world by living as well as they could afford. And as the Melvilles settled down to raise a family, they seemed destined for a rich, comfortable life.

Herman was the Melvilles' third child, born in New York City on August 1, 1819. He had an older brother named Gansevoort and an older sister named Helen. Later, the family grew with the addition of boys named Allan and Thomas and girls named Augusta, Catherine, and Frances. The Melvilles moved several times during Herman's childhood, each time to a bigger and more expensive house, until finally they were living on Broadway, which was then one of New York's most fashionable streets. They had a cook, a nurse, and a governess, and although they could not quite afford to own a carriage and horses, they always hired a carriage when they traveled. Following the custom of well-to-do parents, Allan and Maria Melville sent the children to dancing school. They also sent the boys to private school, starting at the age of seven. There Herman was introduced to literature, history, geography, public speaking, and other subjects.

One shadow over Herman's childhood was the brilliance of his older brother, Gansevoort. It is clear from Allan Melville's letters to family members that Gansevoort was his favorite, and it seems that he showed that favoritism at home. Gansevoort excelled in all subjects at school, while Herman was a more ordinary student. Compared with Gansevoort, Herman seemed to his father to be "very backward in speech and somewhat slow in comprehension," as Allan Melville described the boy in a letter to his in-laws.[1] Other family members, however, found young Herman not at all backward. His grandparents on both sides were especially fond of him, and so were some of his aunts and uncles. On his own part, Herman treated Gansevoort with the normal mischievousness of a younger brother; he teased the older boy whenever Gansevoort showed off, as he frequently did, by reciting poetry to impress the grownups.

Allan Melville as he appeared around 1820, not long after his son Herman was born. His life was a constant struggle to keep up appearances in the face of growing debt.

On the surface, the Melvilles appeared happy and prosperous. But beneath the surface, tensions were building. Herman's mother complained about living in New York, and she also fell into poor health. She grew depressed, began suffering from fainting spells, and spent a growing amount of time in bed. Gansevoort and Herman were sent away from home every summer to stay with relatives, partly because Maria

Melville thought New York in summer was unhealthy for children and partly to protect her delicate nerves from the noise and bustle of active boys.

One of these visits may have helped shape Herman's future. He spent the summer of 1828 with his mother's sister Mary, whose husband, a sea captain named John De Wolf, had made a long voyage to Russia. Herman listened with great excitement to De Wolf's tales of life at sea and visits to far ports. Perhaps Herman's own wanderlust began to stir at that time. His dreams of travel and adventure were also fed by stories about two cousins, Thomas Melville and Guert Gansevoort, who had gone to sea—Guert in the navy and Thomas on a whaling ship. Herman's own father had traveled widely and boasted that he had spent nearly two years of his life on ships, further fueling the boy's interest in travel.

Money was another ever-present problem in the Melville household. There was simply never enough of it. Allan Melville found it increasingly difficult to support his growing family in the style he favored, and his import business was not doing well. It was a time of economic depression in the United States; everybody was feeling the pinch of hard times. People who owed Allan Melville money failed to pay their bills on time, and as a result he could not pay his own debts. More and more often, he had to turn to his father for aid. Major Melville helped as much as he could, until he lost his own job as an official of the Port of Boston. Allan's brother, Thomas Melville, who lived on a farm in Massachusetts, was sued and thrown in jail for debt, and Allan lived in constant dread of the same thing happening to him.

Allan Melville's financial circumstances grew shakier and shakier until, in 1830, they collapsed. He did not have the money to pay a large debt he owed, and he was forced to close his business and move with his family to Albany in northern

New York, leaving behind a stack of unpaid bills. Hoping to make a fresh start in Albany, he rented a house and sent his sons to a highly respected school called the Albany Academy. Gansevoort and young Allan were enrolled in the traditional classical course of study suitable for a gentleman's sons, but Herman's father had decided that his third child's talents were better suited to a career in trade, so Herman was enrolled in the less prestigious commercial course. While his brothers won prizes in Latin composition and ancient history, Herman studied bookkeeping.

Relatives on both the Gansevoort and Melville sides of the family were lending Allan Melville money to pay his expenses while he struggled to get back on his financial feet. Finally, Melville opened a manufacturing plant and store for fur hats, representing a New York City fur company. He invested every cent he could borrow in this costly venture and then, frantic to earn enough money to fend off his creditors, drove himself to the point of exhaustion to get the business started.

In December of 1831, Allan Melville made a business trip to New York City by steamship down the Hudson River. He traveled on deck in the freezing weather because that was the least expensive form of passage. On her return trip, the boat was halted by ice in the river, and Melville completed the journey in open wagons, traveling for several days and nights with the temperature near zero. He returned home ill from exposure, but he refused to rest, insisting that he had to work.

A month later, Melville's health broke down under the strain. He developed pneumonia and also suffered a mental breakdown. Confined at home, he sobbed and screamed during fits of delirium while his children listened in horror. Their father's physical illness was distressing, but they were even more disturbed by his mental instability, which they did not understand. Herman's uncle Thomas came to see his brother and wrote sadly to Judge Lemuel Shaw, a family friend in Boston, that he almost hoped Allan would die, for the doctors claimed that if he survived he would never fully recover his sanity.

Allan Melville's troubles ended on January 28, 1832. He died late at night of pneumonia and was buried three days later. His grieving family, however, could not even mourn their loss in peace. They had no money at all and were immediately confronted with a tangle of problems and difficult decisions. Allan Melville had left his family debts totalling twenty-five thousand dollars, a sum that amounted to a fortune in the 1830s.

Herman Melville was twelve years old when his father died—a formative age, at which children form lasting impressions. He was old enough to be aware of the family's desperate financial straits. He had grown up in a household where the outward appearance of wealth had always been at odds with the inward fears and worries about money. He believed he had seen his father driven to madness and death by his inability to provide for the financial security of his family, and now he felt the shame of the poor relative who must depend on charity from others.

Soon after Allan Melville's death, Herman's mother had a conference with her relatives in which she learned the full extent of her husband's debts and her own precarious financial situation. Her first step was to take the boys out of the expensive Albany Academy and put them to work. Gansevoort, who was sixteen, was put in charge of the fur hat business his father had started. A job was found for Herman as a clerk in a local bank. His first task was to improve his handwriting, for his employers complained that they could not read it.

Throughout the spring of 1832, young Herman struggled to master the skills demanded of him and to adjust to his new circumstances. His future as a bank clerk looked anything but exciting, and deep inside him a seed of restlessness and independence was quietly growing.

2

FIRST
VOYAGE

For several years after his father's death, Herman Melville worked diligently at the bank. At one point, when an epidemic of the deadly disease cholera broke out in Albany, Maria Melville took Herman and her younger children to their uncle Thomas's farm in Pittsfield, in western Massachusetts. Herman also spent his vacations from the bank on this farm, working in the fields and enjoying the view of the gentle Berkshire Mountains from the farmhouse porch. To Herman, Pittsfield became a place of peace and stability. He was saddened when his uncle had to leave the farm and flee to the Illinois prairies to escape his debts.

In the meantime, Gansevoort Melville was trying to restore the family fortunes. At first it seemed that he would be a success in the fur hat business, but in the spring of 1834 a fire destroyed part of the hat factory. To help his brother's firm survive, Herman left the bank in 1835 to work for Gansevoort as a clerk, keeping the books and selling hats in the store that was attached to the factory.

One advantage of working in the family business was that

Herman found a little time now and then to attend classes at the Albany Classical School. Eager to continue his education, he studied mathematics and other subjects, but his professors later remembered that his strongest point had been his writing. He loved writing essays and themes. He also loved reading, and he joined the Albany Young Men's Association for Mutual Improvement, a club that gave him the use of a large library for a fee of two dollars a year. During the mid-1830s, the teenage Herman Melville spent many hours poring over books from the club library. Within a year or two he had received enough education to qualify as a schoolteacher.

Herman was lucky to have his teacher's certificate, for he soon found himself looking for work. Gansevoort Melville, like his father before him, was a victim of economic hard times and his own poor business practices. He was caught up in the panic of 1837, a nationwide economic depression. Hundreds of banks and businesses were forced to close, and thousands of people lost their jobs. Although the Melville family's new troubles were caused primarily by the national economic condition and not completely by mismanagement on the part of Gansevoort Melville, the family was reminded again of how swiftly financial security could disappear. Gansevoort owed large sums of money but could not collect funds from those who owed money to him. As a result, he lost the fur hat firm and had to borrow four thousand dollars from uncle Peter Gansevoort, Maria Melville's brother, to keep creditors from seizing the family's furniture and possessions to pay his debts. Shaken by his failure, Gansevoort went off to New York City to look for a job, and young Allan was taken out of school and put to work as a law clerk. Herman managed to find a job teaching at a country school not far from Pittsfield.

Like most rural schools, Melville's was a small, one-room

building. Melville boarded at a farm a mile and a half from the school, atop what he called a "savage and lonely" mountain. On his first day in the new job, the inexperienced teacher was confronted with thirty students of all ages and levels of skill. Some were his age; a few were utterly illiterate. In such extreme conditions Melville found it hard to maintain discipline, let alone teach. After six weeks he gave up the job in disgust and returned to Albany.

For a few months Melville looked for work without success. His leisure hours, though, were filled with excitement. Early in 1838 he organized a debating club and promptly got into a dispute over the presidency of the club with a rival member. Their argument was reported in a local paper called the *Albany Microscope*, which published some of Melville's letters—his first appearance in print.

Before long Maria Melville was forced to admit that she could no longer afford to live in Albany. Faced with the prospect of having constantly to ask her brother Peter for money to buy coal and flour and to pay her bills, she finally decided to move her family to Lansingburgh, a village not far from Albany on the banks of the Hudson River. There the Melvilles could live more cheaply than in Albany. They settled into a rented house in Lansingburgh in May of 1838.

Herman Melville was in a difficult and unhappy position. Although he was almost twenty years old—an adult by the standards of the day—he was not contributing to his family's income and felt ashamed. At the same time, he was unable to decide on a career or even settle down to a job. Upstate New York was in the grip of an economic depression and offered few career opportunities—except one. The state was widening and deepening the Erie Canal, the artificial waterway that linked the Hudson River with Lake Erie, and there was work for skilled surveyors and engineers.

Maria Melville, Herman's mother, was a strong-willed, rather overbearing woman who sometimes tried to manage her son's life.

Melville signed up for a scientific course at the Lansing-burgh Academy in the hope of preparing himself for a survey-ing job. He also asked his uncle to intervene on his behalf, and Peter Gansevoort urged the canal commissioners to hire the young man as a surveyor. While he was waiting to hear about a job on the canal, Melville amused himself by writing two humorous essays for the Lansingburgh paper. They were published under the title "Fragments from a Writing Desk" in the spring of 1839. By this time, Melville realized that he was not going to get a job on the canal. He began casting about for something—anything—to do.

Melville was now fully grown, a slightly stocky young man five feet nine inches tall, with thick brown hair, a straight nose, and rather small blue eyes. At some point in his early manhood he grew a thick, bushy beard, which he wore without a mustache in the fashion of the time (later on he wore a mustache as well). The young Herman Melville was neither handsome nor distinguished, but he was pleasant looking. He had an air of quiet thoughtfulness that people noticed and remembered. Above all, he was healthy and strong and eager to see the world outside the narrow boundaries of the life he had known. Perhaps because he remembered the stories of his uncle and his two cousins who had gone to sea, Melville made up his mind to try his own fate at sea. He asked his brother Gansevoort to look for a ship's berth for him, and almost immediately he was hired as a crewman aboard the *St. Lawrence*, a three-masted merchant ship that was preparing to cross the Atlantic Ocean from New York City to Liverpool, England. The ship carried a cargo of cotton—the bounty of the South's cotton fields bound for England's textile mills.

The *St. Lawrence* sailed from New York on June 3, 1839. Melville could take pride in the fact that he was earning his own living at last. But as he was about to discover, life aboard a nineteenth-century sailing vessel was not entirely a carefree adventure. There were many dangerous, unpleasant, even horrible aspects to the seafaring life.

Melville quickly learned humility. He was both better educated than most of his shipmates and older than many of the common, or unskilled, seamen, yet he knew nothing at all about ships or sailing. He had to learn a whole new language, in which every rope, every task, and every part of the ship and its complicated rigging had a special name. He learned too about the strict discipline of the sea, which required him to address the officers respectfully and to follow their orders unquestioningly. Furthermore, he had to endure the practical jokes, sarcasm, and often cruel humor of the more experienced crewmen, who traditionally made life difficult for "green" hands on their first voyage.

The duties of the common seaman were demanding. On his very first day, Melville learned to scamper aloft into the web of ropes and spars that stretched high above the deck. There, clinging with his legs to a swaying wooden crosspiece or a rope at least six stories above the rolling deck or the sea, he would haul on a section of the immense canvas sail and then race down a rope ladder for his next order. It was not unknown for even experienced seamen to fall to their deaths from the uncertain footing of the rigging.

When they were not hauling the sails up or down, the crewmen were kept busy with other tasks. Among the most hated of these were chipping rust from the anchor chains, scraping the decks clean, and repainting sections of the hull that had blistered from the effects of sun, rain, and salt water. Sailors had few idle moments, and those moments had to be spent in a small, stuffy part of the ship called the forecastle. Crowded with bunks and sea chests, stale with the odors of tobacco and unwashed men, the forecastle was where the crew slept, ate, and occasionally tried to relax. Meals were always eagerly awaited, although the food was monotonous and not very good: cornmeal mush, salted beef, hard biscuit, and coffee, with molasses pudding on Sundays as a treat.

Despite the grueling work and grim conditions of life on the *St. Lawrence*, Melville found enjoyment in his new job. It was satisfying to master new skills and new knowledge, and there was an undeniable thrill in being aloft in the rigging during rough weather. He later wrote in *Redburn: His First Voyage*:

> *There was a wild delirium about it; a fine rushing of the blood about the heart; and a glad thrilling and throbbing of the whole system, to find yourself tossed up at every pitch into the clouds of a stormy sky, and hovering like a judgment angel between heaven and earth; both hands free, with one foot in the rigging, and one somewhere behind you in the air.*[1]

The sea itself offered fascinating new sights: the glowing wake left by the ship at night as it plowed its way through masses of tiny phosphorescent creatures, the pods of porpoises that leaped and dove on either side, and the endless rise and fall of the surging, soothing waves. But Melville was disappointed in his first glimpses of foreign lands. Ireland was nothing more than a blur of clouds on the horizon, and the hills of Wales just looked like his home in New York State. He was amazed and impressed, however, by the sights that greeted him when the *St. Lawrence* reached port in Liverpool. He thought he had seen a big, important port in New York City, but Liverpool made New York seem tiny and insignificant.

In the mid-nineteenth century, Liverpool was the largest and busiest port in the world. Each year more than 1,500 ships tied up at the 14 huge docks that covered 90 acres of its waterfront. Vessels from the United States docked next to ships from every seagoing nation, even occasional high-prowed native junks from China. All around, ships' masts rose like the trees in a dense forest. High stone walls separated the docks from the rest of the city, and sailors going in and out had to pass through customs checkpoints to prevent

*Tea chests being unloaded on the Liverpool docks. Melville's first voyage took
him to the world's busiest port—and one of its worst slums.*

the smuggling of goods off the ships.

The *St. Lawrence* remained in port for six weeks while the
crew unloaded cotton and took on a new cargo. During this
time, the crew boarded at a sailors' lodging house in the city.
Melville had to return to the ship to work for part of each day
except Sunday, but he was free to spend his evenings seeing
the sights. There was much to see.

At the time of Melville's visit, Liverpool was growing fast.
People straggled into the city from the famine-stricken farms
of Ireland, the poor mining towns of Wales, and the English
countryside, all seeking jobs in the city's factories or docks.
But work was scarce, and many people remained unemployed.
They settled into vast, teeming slums unlike anything that
yet existed in America. Nearly 20,000 people lived in dark,

damp cellars in the Liverpool slums, and the same number or more lived in squalid, filthy tenements. Wandering innocently into the slums, Melville was appalled at the sight of beggars, prostitutes, drunkards, and ragged children living in conditions worse than any he had ever imagined.

Years later, in his novel *Redburn*, Melville described an incident in the slums of Liverpool that may have been based on a real life experience. Redburn, the book's narrator, told of passing through a dingy alley and hearing "a feeble wail, which seemed to come out of the earth." It was "the low, hopeless, endless wail of some one forever lost." Peering into a deep, crumbling cellar beneath a warehouse, he made out "the figure of what had once been a woman," clutching the still, shrunken bodies of her children.[2] For two days Redburn tried to get help for them, but neither the police, nor the factory watchman across the street, nor the landlady at his lodging house offered any assistance. He returned to the cellar on the third day only to be greeted by the smell of death and the sight of a glistening pile of quicklime, a chemical in which the bodies of paupers were buried.

Melville realized that his own family's poverty would be considered wealth by the pathetic slum dwellers of Liverpool. He also formed a powerfully negative impression of modern industrial "civilization." He asked himself how a nation as rich and powerful as Great Britain could allow such horrors to continue. In *Redburn*, he wrote, "I stood looking down on them while my whole soul swelled within me; and I asked myself, What right had any body in the wide world to smile and be glad, when sights like this were to be seen?"[3]

He tried, however, to absorb some happier, more instructive sights during his first trip abroad. Soon after arriving in Liverpool he bought a guidebook to the city. The book happened to be thirty years old, and Melville amused himself with the notion that his father might have used that same guidebook on his own long-ago visit to Liverpool. With the book as his guide, Melville dutifully took a number of walks through the city, admiring its fine public buildings. But he missed his family, and in a letter to his mother he wrote that he would exchange all the fine sights he had seen for a glimpse of "a corner of home."[4] Throughout his life Melville was to be pulled by the same opposing forces: He wanted to see the world, but once he was far from home he felt unbearably homesick for his loved ones.

The trip from Liverpool back to New York was uneventful. Melville had performed his duties competently enough and could no doubt have signed on for another voyage, but for the time being he had lost interest in the sailor's life. Instead, he headed for home.

Arriving in Lansingburgh after an absence of four months, Melville found that his family's money troubles had grown even worse. Threatened with the sale of her furniture by her creditors, Maria Melville again appealed to her brothers Peter and Herman Gansevoort for help. And again Herman's uncles, who were having their own financial problems at the time, tided their sister over with enough money to pay the most pressing bills. Despite their generosity, Maria complained bitterly that her relatives and friends did not do enough for her. She demanded a regular allowance from them, and she even threatened to break up her family and send her children to live with various aunts and uncles.

The Melvilles' financial affairs seemed more hopeless than ever. On top of everything else, Gansevoort, the oldest son, was ill and unable to work. Young Allan was working as a law clerk, but he did not yet earn enough money to support himself, much less add to the family income. Herman

Melville was once more faced with a burden of responsibility. Although he did not yet know what he wanted to do with his life, he knew he had to do something to earn his own living, and, if possible, to help his mother.

3

THE RESTLESS SEARCHER

Melville was determined to find work, but he had few choices. Reluctantly, he decided to return to teaching and found a job at the Greenbush Academy, not far from Lansingburgh. Fortunately, Greenbush turned out to be a much more congenial place than the country school where Melville had had his first teaching experience. As one of several teachers at Greenbush, Melville had fewer students and less responsibility than in the earlier position. He was able to return to writing and published a story in the Lansingburgh paper in November of 1839. At Greenbush Melville also made a new friend, a young man named Eli James Murdock Fly. Melville may have been romantically attracted to Fly's sister Harriet, for she signed her name and wrote comments in a book he owned, and he apparently visited her home often. If there was a romance, however, it faded. Melville's own prospects were far too troubled for him to think about marriage.

When he took the job at Greenbush, Melville had proudly promised his mother that he would be able to give her $150 or even $200 from his earnings over the school year. As time went on, however, he realized with a sinking heart that he could not keep that promise. The school failed to pay him the salary it owed him; in fact, Greenbush ran out of money and closed in May of 1840. At the end of a year of teaching, Melville was left to walk home with only $3 in his pocket, not the $150 he had hoped to provide.

His failure to keep his pledge of support, even though it was not his fault, ate into Melville's spirit. He grew with-drawn and depressed, refusing even to open his mail. Looking around him, he saw that employment opportunities were still scarce in New York State. Another teaching job—even if he had been able to find one—might have resulted only in another disappointment or disaster. Melville decided to do what many Americans before him, including his uncle Thomas Melville, had done. He would "turn his face to the great West," as newspaper editor Horace Greeley put it in 1855. Greeley, who founded the *New York Tribune* in 1841 and played an important part in American political and intel-lectual life in the mid-nineteenth century, advised his readers to seek their fortunes on the American frontier. The West seemed to offer a fresh start, free of the financial woes and stagnation of the eastern cities.

Melville's friend Fly was also feeling discouraged and rest-less. He eagerly agreed to join Melville in a westward journey. In June of 1840 the two set out for Galena, Illinois, on the edge of the Great Plains. A few years earlier, Thomas Melville had established himself in Galena, and the young men thought that he might help them get started in business there.

The first stage of their trip took them along the Erie Canal, where Melville had once hoped in vain for a job as a surveyor. At one point the Canal ran past the site of old Fort

Stanwix. Melville made a point of examining the place where his grandfather Gansevoort had distinguished himself during the American Revolution and where he had been presented with a captured British drum as a trophy.

The Erie Canal was a bustling, exciting, even dangerous place that ran for more than 350 miles from Albany west to Buffalo. It was crowded with hundreds of eighty-foot-long canal boats that carried cargo and immigrants from the East Coast to the Great Lakes, the gateway to the frontier. Mules and horses plodded along towpaths on either side of the canal, hauling the boats. Travelers who did not want to pay for a fare on the passenger boats could also make their way along the towpaths, getting rides from friendly canalmen whenever possible and walking between rides. In later years, Melville said that he had once been a "vagabond" along the Erie Canal, so he and Fly probably walked the towpaths. If so, they risked perils more serious than sore feet, for gangs of thieves and ruffians roamed the verges of the canals, especially in a notorious stretch of swampland between the cities of Syracuse and Rochester. It may have been there that they ran into trouble and were lucky enough to get out of it, for Melville later referred to an honest canalman who lent a strong arm to defend a poor stranger in time of danger.

Although they left no record of it, Melville and Fly may have visited Niagara Falls near the western end of the canal; the Falls were already becoming a tourist attraction. Melville did record his astonishment at the colorful mix of people he saw in the streets of Buffalo—uniformed soldiers, rugged backwoodsmen dressed in skins, lady tourists carefully holding their skirts out of the mud, Native Americans in deerskin trousers with babies strapped to their backs, French and Canadian visitors from across the nearby border with Canada, and immigrants from Ireland and Germany pushing westward.

It was a scene of furious activity, much of it centered around the Lake Erie wharves, where steamboats took on passengers for the week-long trip through the Great Lakes to Chicago. Melville and his companion paid ten dollars each for a ticket on one of these lake steamers.

They discovered that the Great Lakes could be just as rough as any ocean. During one storm, the cold waters were so choppy that even seasoned passengers like Melville—and also some horses that had been brought aboard—were seasick. However, most of the trip was quieter and more interesting. The steamer chugged through Lake Erie, stopping at Cleveland, and then through Lake Huron, where the wilderness began. Melville gazed at what he called the "ancient and unentered forests" along the shore and occasionally saw Indians skimming the waves in birchbark canoes.

At Mackinac Island, where Lake Huron meets Lake Michigan between the peninsulas of upper and lower Michigan, the travelers went ashore briefly. They explored the fort that crowned the heights, once a vital point in the defense of the old Northwest Territory, and the Indian settlements on the beach. The steamboat then made its way south through Lake Michigan to the biggest town in the region, Chicago. In just seven years, Chicago had grown from a rough settlement of a fort and three houses to an inland port of seven thousand inhabitants. Its hotels, warehouses, stagecoach firms, and stables catered to the steady flow of travelers headed west.

Melville and Fly hired horses for the three-day trip from Chicago to Galena. Melville never forgot that ride. The wild prairie was like an ocean of grass, reaching as high as his saddle and rolling in gentle waves to the horizon. Red, purple, yellow, and blue wildflowers bloomed everywhere, striping the prairie like a rainbow. Melville later recalled his wonderment as he waded knee-deep through fields of brilliant orange tiger lilies.

Arriving in Galena, Melville and his friend found to their disappointment that their prospects for work were no better than they had been in New York. The economic depression that troubled the East had reached to the frontier states, and Thomas Melville was unable to help the two job seekers. He barely made enough money to support his family.

Melville and Fly looked around for a month or so, then faced the sad fact that Illinois had nothing to offer them. They could have gone farther west, across the Mississippi River into the Missouri Territory or even on to California or Oregon as many pioneers were doing in the 1840s, but there is no evidence that they ever considered such an idea. In the early autumn, they turned back toward New York State and home.

They did not retrace their steps, however. Instead of going back across the Great Lakes and down the Erie Canal, they embarked on the other great waterway of the central United States: the Mississippi River, which flowed south past Galena. They took passage on a riverboat, stopping briefly at St. Louis, Missouri, in order to see the sights of that frontier town, the starting point for many journeys of exploration in the West. At the southern border of Illinois, Melville and Fly left the Mississippi to travel eastward up the Ohio River, but their few days on the Mississippi had given Melville memories that he would use in books and poems decades later.

Melville did not leave a clear record of the end of this journey, but he and Fly probably left the Ohio River in western Pennsylvania to travel overland through the Allegheny Mountains to Philadelphia. By mid-November they had reached New York City. There Melville found his older brother Gansevoort, still in poor health, studying law. The two wanderers lodged in a cheap boardinghouse and looked for jobs. Gansevoort helped them out by paying for their meals; they ate at an inexpensive restaurant where a plate of meat cost six cents and vegetables three cents. "They are both in good health and tolerable spirits," reported Gansevoort in a letter to his mother.[1]

Fly eventually found work as a copyist, making copies of manuscripts and documents—a necessary job in the age before photography and photocopying. Melville was not so lucky. His handwriting was still hard to read, so he could not work as a copyist. He did not want to return home because he knew that he could not find work in Albany or Lansingburgh. Moreover, he did not want to be a burden on his mother, who continued to borrow money from her brothers to support herself and her daughters. He began to think of going to sea again—to the Pacific Ocean this time.

Several things might have helped turn Melville's thoughts to the Pacific. While visiting with his uncle Thomas Melville, he must have talked about his cousin, Thomas's son, who had become a whaler in the Pacific. Although the family worried about this cousin, who had become an alcoholic and lost contact with his relatives, there was nevertheless something stirring about his wild, independent life. Also, during Melville's stay in Galena, the family had discussed a local newspaper article about the remarkable adventures of an American sailor who had been held captive for nearly twenty years by the native people of Timor, an island north of Australia. Around this same time, Melville had read two novels about seafaring exploits: *Two Years Before the Mast* (1840), by Richard Henry Dana, and *The Red Rover* (1828), by James Fenimore Cooper. All these stories stimulated Melville's restless imagination, until in December of 1840 he decided to sign on to a whaling ship.

This was a much more momentous undertaking than his earlier summer voyage to Liverpool and back. Whaling ships were generally away from their home ports for years at a time. Whaling was a dangerous activity—there were any number of ways in which a whaler could be killed or mutilated. Furthermore, whaling was much less respectable than serving in a naval or merchant vessel. Although the captains and owners of whaling ships were people of some standing in their communities, many whalers' crews were drawn from the dregs of the sailing community—illiterates, criminals, troublemakers, and the riffraff of a score of foreign ports.

Yet Melville's decision made sense to him. He would be occupied and fed for as long as the voyage lasted; he would receive a small salary; and if the ship returned with a large cargo of whale oil he would be given a share of the profits. At the same time, he would see one of the most remote and exotic parts of the world: the South Pacific, called by many people the South Seas.

He went to Lansingburgh to spend Christmas with his family, regaling his sisters with accounts of his western trip and talk of the exciting things he would see in the Pacific Islands—"the Cannibal Isles," as the girls said with a shudder and a laugh.

On December 31, 1840, Melville signed on as a common seaman aboard the *Acushnet*, a brand-new whaling ship registered in New Bedford, Massachusetts. He was given eighty-four dollars for signing, but most of that money had to go toward the purchase of clothing, blankets, a straw-filled mattress for his narrow bunk in the forecastle, a knife, and other items he would need during the voyage. For the next few days, while the ship's hold was being filled with supplies, he roamed the streets of the busy port, soaking up the atmosphere of a community built on commercial whaling. He saw the Whaleman's Chapel; he saw the crews of other whalers go aboard their ships; and he watched a steady stream of ships head out to sea.

The years 1835–40 were the peak of the American whaling industry. About 750 whaling ships operated out of various New England ports, and in any one season as many as 500 of them were likely to be hunting in the Pacific. Each whaler had a crew of around forty men. Their chief prey was the sperm whale, hunted throughout the world's oceans but mostly in the South and Central Pacific. The whaling grounds of the North Pacific, in the waters off Japan, were just beginning to be opened up at the time of Melville's voyage.

Whaling was a major business. In the decades before the birth of the petroleum industry in the 1860s, whale oil was highly prized as lamp fuel. It was obtained by cutting the fatty flesh of whales into large chunks that were cooked in huge kettles called try-pots until the oil ran out and could be captured in barrels. Sperm whales were especially prized because, in addition to the oil in their flesh, their heads contained huge cavities filled with a particularly pure oil called spermaceti. Some sperm whales offered still another valuable product. Their intestines contained lumps of a rare substance called ambergris that they had secreted to coat the sharp, indigestible beaks of squid. Ambergris was used in the making of perfume and was one of the most precious commodities in the world—worth its weight in gold.

Each year during the mid-nineteenth century, the whaling fleets of the United States, England, Russia, Norway, and other nations grew larger. Whalers probed the earth's waters from Antarctica to the Arctic. Before long, the whales of

In huge kettles called try-pots, whale blubber was melted into oil. When whales were plentiful, the fires roared night and day, and the greasy smoke covered the ship and everything in it.

many species that had once roamed the seas in huge numbers were hunted almost to extinction. As early as 1845, the sperm whale population had dropped dramatically, and by 1890 the gray whale was thought to be extinct (although a few gray whales survived to keep the species alive). But when the *Acushnet* sailed out of New Bedford harbor on January 3, 1841, Herman Melville knew nothing of the whale's threatened future, or of the whaling industry that would one day form the subject of his greatest novel.

4

"AMONG THE CANNIBALS"

At first, Melville congratulated himself upon his choice of the *Acushnet*. This was the ship's first voyage, so everything aboard was clean and new, although Melville soon learned that nothing dirtied a ship and its crew more quickly than whaling. The crew was a bit more mature and better educated than the average whaleship crew, and in addition to the usual foreigners there were a number of New Englanders with whom Melville felt at home. The ship was even equipped with a library for the men's use, and the captain, Valentine Pease, seemed both reasonable and capable.

The voyage began well. The *Acushnet* sailed south through the Atlantic with a man posted high on the tallest mast to look for whales. When he spotted the spray from a whale's blowhole, he would cry out, "Blo-o-o-w! Thar he blows!" and the crew would leap into action. Five-hundred-pound whaleboats were lowered over the side of the ship, each manned by one of the ship's mates, four oarsmen, and a harpooner. Each boat contained a four-hundred-yard reel of

"The South Sea Whale Fishery," painted by Louis Garneray. From his shipmates, Melville heard lurid tales of boats crushed and men killed by whales in their death throes.

rope to which the harpoon was attached.

After chasing their prey, sometimes for hours on end under the burning tropical sun, the oarsmen would row as close as possible to the whale—within arm's length, if they could—so that the harpooner could plunge his steel harpoon into the whale's flesh. As soon as he struck, the real danger began. The whale might take off for the horizon as fast as it could, pulling the boat along behind in what the whalemen called a "Nantucket sleigh-ride" (many whalers were from Nantucket). Or the whale might "sound," raising its powerful tail high above the boat for a plunge straight down into the depths. Whaleboats were sometimes crushed by the tails of sounding whales. If the harpoon had gravely wounded it, the whale might go into a dying "flurry," thrashing about wildly in the water and putting the boat at risk of being swamped or smashed. But whatever happened, the boatmen were attached to the whale by the line, which itself was a threat. As the line whipped off its reel down the middle of the boat, the oarsmen had to be careful to stay clear of it no matter how the boat was tossing, for it could tear off a limb or drag a man to death by drowning in an instant if he were careless enough to let it touch him.

However long it took—and it sometimes took several days—the duty of the boatmen was to stay with the whale until the mate could get close enough to deliver a deathblow with his sharp eight-foot lance (the harpoon alone usually did not kill the whale). Then, once the battle was done, the boatmen towed the whale back to the ship where they lashed its carcass to the hull and immediately began the task of "trying-out" the flesh, or rendering it into oil. The huge try-pots on the deck were uncovered, and men armed with razor-sharp flensing knives, which were used to strip whales, descended onto a narrow, slippery platform to begin cutting up the carcass. Their job may have seemed less glamorous than that of the harpooner, but it was equally risky. The slightest misstep could cause them to be crushed between the carcass and the ship's hull, gashed by a knife, or thrown into the sea where sharks always swarmed to tear at the carcass. Covered with blood and grease, the cutters hacked the whale into long strips that were raised on hooks and sliced into smaller pieces, called bible-leaves, for the try-pots. Fires burned under the pots for hours as the flesh was melted down into oil, and the ship, the sails, and all the men were coated with slimy, evil-smelling black soot. All the while, they hoped for another cry of "Thar he blows!" so that the whole process could start over again.

Although the *Acushnet*, like most New England whalers, was bound for the Pacific whaling grounds, it managed to capture several whales in the Atlantic. After two months of sailing, when the ship reached Rio de Janeiro, Brazil, it had 150 barrels of oil in its hold. These were transferred to another New England vessel to be shipped home, and the *Acushnet* left Rio after only a single day in the scenic port that Melville called "the bay of all beauties." The captain turned the ship southward toward Cape Horn at the tip of South America. The passage around the Cape was one of the most treacherous in the world because of the almost constant storms and unpredictable winds that raged there. As they approached Cape Horn, also called the Cape of Storms, Melville heard many dire stories from his fellow crewmen about these wild southern waters.

The men also told whaling tales, of course. Some of these tales concerned an unusual sperm whale called Mocha Dick. Unusually pale—almost white in patches—Mocha Dick lived in the Pacific and was said to be aggressive, unlike ordinary sperm whales. Mocha Dick, the sailors swore, chased whale-boats. This whale had grown so famous that an article about him appeared in the *Knickerbocker*, a New York magazine of the 1840s and 1850s. Melville probably read the article, which appeared not long before the *Acushnet* sailed.

Even more famous was the story of the *Essex*, a whaleship that had met a strange fate in 1819. A sperm whale had smashed in the hull of the *Essex*, which sank in just ten min-utes. Owen Chase, a New Englander who was first mate of the *Essex* and who survived the tragedy, wrote an account of the event in which he claimed that the whale had deliber-ately and furiously attacked the ship in revenge for the har-pooning of three other whales. All over the world, whalemen argued about Chase's story. Some believed that a whale *could* be intelligent and even vengeful; others claimed that the sinking of the *Essex* was just bad luck and that the whale did not know what it was doing.

Melville listened to these discussions with great interest, and he was even more fascinated when he learned that one of his shipmates aboard the *Acushnet* had sailed several times with Owen Chase. Later, when the *Acushnet* stopped to exchange news with another ship, Melville learned that Chase's son was aboard the vessel and was allowed to meet the boy and read his copy of his father's book. Owen Chase was becoming a heroic figure to Melville, and the idea of deliberate, personal combat between a man and a whale had lodged in his imagination.

The voyage continued. The passage around the Cape, despite the dreadful tales Melville had heard, was not too bad. The *Acushnet* was buffeted by a gale for three or four days but managed to round the Cape into the wide Pacific without serious trouble or loss of life. The ship then headed north into warmer waters along the west coast of South America. It passed Más a Tierra, a tiny island off the coast of Chile that was famous to both sailors and readers as Robinson Crusoe's Island. In 1704, a Scottish seaman named Alexander Selkirk had been marooned on Más a Tierra by his companions; later his adventures formed the basis of Daniel Defoe's popular 1719 novel *Robinson Crusoe*. A few days after passing the island, the boats of the *Acushnet* were lowered for the first time in the Pacific to chase sperm whales off the coast of Valparaiso, Chile.

When the *Acushnet* docked at Santa Marta, Peru, in June of 1841, Melville wrote to his brother Gansevoort that he was well pleased with the voyage so far. His shipmates, he declared, were "much superior in morale and early advantages to the ordinary run of a whaling crew," and he had enjoyed seeing a little of South America. But apparently one of Melville's fellow crewmen was less happy on the *Acushnet*, for he deserted—an ominous hint of things to come.

Yet all continued well for a while after the *Acushnet* left Santa Marta. By late September, more than 450 of the ship's 2,800 barrels were full of oil; counting the 150 sent home from Rio, nearly a quarter of the barrels had been filled. The date October 1, 1841, was a memorable one since the hunting that day kept the fires burning under the try-pots for days and yielded 100 barrels of oil. Captain and crew alike felt optimistic, for the winter, which lay ahead, was believed to be the best hunting season. It seemed that they might fill as many as half their barrels in the next few months.

Suddenly, however, their luck changed. Day after day the lookout scanned the horizon but saw no sign of whales. Captain Pease ordered the ship to the Galápagos Islands, where whales were often to be found, but other whalers they met there told the same sad story: no whales. Nevertheless, Melville was glad of a chance to see the Galápagos, with their arid, rocky landscapes and giant, slow-moving tortoises. The Galápagos were called the Encantadas, or Enchanted Islands, because their tricky currents made it difficult to navigate among them. Mariners sometimes claimed that the islands seemed to jump about as if by magic. Years later Melville would write several stories about the Encantadas.

In the months that followed, Captain Pease drove the *Acushnet* on a zigzag course along the northwest coast of South America and back again through the Galápagos Islands, but to no avail. Several times the lookout spotted whales, but the boats proved unable to make a kill. In January of 1842, Pease gave up on the coastal waters—the on-shore grounds, as whalers called them—and ordered the ship west into the off-shore grounds of the open Pacific.

et's luck continued to be poor. The cap-
v whaler they met out at sea complained
usually scarce and hard to catch.
en had not yet realized it, the sperm
emely scarce, and the survivors were
verhunting had taken its toll. Between Jan-
ay, the *Acushnet* sighted 9 groups of whales but
only 2 or 3 kills, adding a mere 150 barrels of oil to its
cargo. In June the men killed another whale—another 50
barrels. It now looked as though it would take them years to
fill all 2,800 barrels. Their chance to make a quick, record-
setting voyage had evaporated.

The run of bad luck soured Captain Pease's disposition.
Not only was he annoyed at the lack of whales, he was also
suffering from poor health. This was to have been his last
voyage, and he had planned to retire on his profits. With
every week that passed, his retirement drew further off and
his potential profits shrank. He became snappish, strict, and
quarrelsome—so much so that both his first and third mates
were later to leave the ship in disgust. Stress appeared among
the crew as well, as men began to fall ill with scurvy, a vita-
min-deficiency disease caused by a lack of fresh food in the
diet. Fights and feuds broke out, and Melville no longer
rejoiced in the high quality of his shipmates. As soon as Captain Pease took the *Acushnet* south to the Marquesas Islands
to stock up on fresh water and food, Melville began making
plans to depart both ship and captain.

In later years, Melville explained his desertion by saying
that he had run away from the brutal cruelty of the captain.
But there is no evidence that Pease was particularly cruel, or
that Melville suffered any real mistreatment on the *Acushnet*.
From all accounts, Pease was moody, temperamental, and
domineering, but not evil or brutal. Melville's decision to

desert the ship was probably based as much on distaste for whaling and on curiosity about South Seas island life as it was on the need to escape an unbearable situation.

The *Acushnet* anchored in Anna Maria Bay at Nuku Hiva in the Marquesas Islands. Nuku Hiva was especially interesting to Melville because his seagoing cousin Thomas had visited the island thirteen years before and had spent some time with Marquesan villagers—a fact that perhaps convinced Herman Melville that he could do the same thing. When Melville discovered that a fellow crewman named Richard Tobias Greene, or Toby, was also thinking of leaving the ship, he revealed his own plans. The two decided to desert together.

They waited until the captain was ready to put out to sea because, if they deserted too early, Pease could offer the Marquesans cloth, or perhaps even a rifle, in exchange for the return of the deserters. Melville and Toby would certainly be hunted down and brought back to the ship in disgrace. But if they waited until Pease was impatient to get back to the whaling grounds, there was a chance that he would not pursue them very energetically. As for what they planned to do after the ship had sailed away, Melville does not seem to have given much thought to the future. No doubt he expected to stay in a Marquesan village for a time and then leave the island with one of the ships that regularly stopped in the islands for provisions and recreation. Certainly he did not expect to have any difficulty finding a way off the island.

The escape did not go as smoothly as Melville and Toby had planned. First, they were seen by their shipmates as they scrambled up the ridge, and they worried about pursuit. (In fact, Captain Pease did try to trick them—he sailed out of the bay but then hid the ship behind a neighboring island for a day, hoping that the deserters would come down to the beach where they could be recaptured. When the trick failed, he gave up and sailed away.) Second, Melville and Toby had to spend several uncomfortable nights high in the rugged mountains without much food. Third, Melville's injured leg caused delays. And fourth, when they finally did descend into a valley, they wound up going where they least wanted to go: into the home of the Taipis, the much-feared cannibal tribe whom Melville was to call the Typees.

Toby and Melville did not know it was the Taipi valley at first. It was merely a refuge from the inhospitable mountaintops. But reaching the valley floor was no easy task. There was no clearly marked path down from the peaks, so the deserters decided to follow a stream. They did not know it, but this was probably the most difficult route they could have chosen, for the stream leaped down the steep mountainside in a series of waterfalls. Melville and Toby spent three days working their way over slippery rocks and around waterfalls and three nights tossing and turning fretfully in the rain-soaked forest. At last they reached the valley floor, dotted with villages—only to learn to their alarm that they were among the Taipis, the eaters of human flesh.

In later years, Melville said ruefully that he was destined to go down in history as "the man who had lived among the cannibals." But were the Taipis really cannibals? Anthropologists have argued that question for decades. During this century, it has become fashionable among some scholars to dismiss earlier accounts of cannibalism and other so-called primitive behavior as figments of the imaginations of European explorers and travelers, who often believed the worst of native peoples and who often misinterpreted what they saw. Yet sometimes the observations of the early explorers *were* true, and customs among many tribal peoples included behavior that was far removed from European norms.

After the passage of so many years, it is impossible to say whether or not the Taipis among whom Herman Melville found himself in 1842 actually were cannibals. But it is known that some Polynesian peoples, including some inhabitants of the Marquesas Islands, did practice cannibalism well into the nineteenth century, often as a form of religious ritual, in which the flesh of slain enemies was consumed. Norwegian anthropologist and explorer Thor Heyerdahl visited Nuku Hiva and other Marquesan islands in the 1930s, nearly a century after Melville's visit, and reported that there were old people still alive who remembered acts of ritual cannibalism from their younger days.

Even if the Taipis were cannibals, as Melville certainly believed, it is unlikely that he was in any real danger of being killed and eaten. But the fear preyed on his mind during the month he spent among them, and his later descriptions of native life show that he paid especially close attention to everything connected with cooking and eating. He was on the alert for any food that looked suspiciously like "long pig," as some island people called human flesh.

Despite Melville's uneasiness, the Taipis were fairly gracious hosts. They washed, clothed, and fed him and Toby, and gave them a large bamboo hut to live in. But the Taipis would not allow their white visitors to roam freely through the valley. The two deserters had not been settled in the chief Taipi village for very long before they started to wonder how—or if—they would ever leave.

Melville remained discreetly quiet about one aspect of his sojourn in Nuku Hiva. At that time, sex played a part in almost all encounters between whites and Polynesians. Ever since the first European ships had landed in Tahiti in the late eighteenth century, white sailors had been astonished and delighted by the willingness of the island women to engage in sexual relations with them. In Polynesian culture, sex was not regarded as something shameful or secret, and women as well as men were free to offer their sexual favors as they pleased. This openness was their undoing, however, for a great number of the European and American sailors who eagerly embraced Polynesian girls were afflicted with syphilis and other venereal diseases. Soon these diseases were running rampant through the Pacific islanders, killing many of them.

When Melville was in the Marquesas, Christian missionaries had not yet reached these remote islands, and traditional customs—including sexual customs—flourished unchecked. It would not have been surprising if Melville and Toby had enjoyed sexual relationships with women in the Taipi village. The book Melville later wrote about his experience in Nuku Hiva features a beautiful, romantic island girl with the rather improbable name of Fayaway, but this does not necessarily mean that Melville had a romance with a real-life Fayaway.

At any rate, he had other concerns. His status and Toby's status were not very clear. Were they guests of the Taipis, or prisoners? Melville's injured leg seems to have developed an infection, and after several weeks the Taipis allowed Toby to leave the valley and go back to Anna Maria Bay to see if there was a ship there from which he could get medicine for Melville's leg. But Toby did not return. His disappearance was a mystery, and not until many months later did Melville learn that Toby had been seized by a shorthanded whaling ship and forced to join its crew.

While Melville languished in the Taipi village, worrying about Toby's fate and wondering what his own fate would be, word reached Anna Maria Bay that a white man was being held captive by the Taipis. The captain of the *Lucy Ann*, an Australian whaling ship, needed more crewmen, and he sent a boatful of men to rescue Melville. Later, Melville wrote a highly dramatic account of a hairbreadth escape from the savage Taipis, but this was almost certainly an exaggeration. The details of the "escape" are not very convincing, and it is possible that the Taipis did not really exert themselves to keep Melville from leaving them. One way or another, however, in August of 1842 Melville found himself out of the Taipi village and on board the *Lucy Ann*. He had moved from a difficult situation into a new kind of misery.

The *Lucy Ann*, it turned out, was in worse shape than the *Acushnet*. The ship was crowded and filthy; Captain Henry Ventom was ill and incompetent; and the first mate was a drunkard. Conditions aboard the ship were so bad that two officers and seven crewmen had deserted just a short time before, and two other crewmen had been arrested for mutiny and turned over to French officials. While the ship was anchored at Nuku Hiva, three more men tried to desert, but failed. Ventom was reduced to searching the Marquesas for beachcombers and deserters to replenish the *Lucy Ann*'s crew. This was the unhappy and argumentative ship's company that Melville had joined.

Leaving the Marquesas, the *Lucy Ann* made its way to Tahiti and anchored in the harbor at Papeete, Tahiti's capital and one of the chief ports of the South Pacific. The British medical officer in Papeete ordered Captain Ventom off the ship for medical treatment, and a few days later the *Lucy Ann* set out on a short whaling cruise under the command of James German, the first mate.

It was not long before the tensions aboard the ship erupted into open defiance. Several men who had been identified as sick or injured by the medical officer in Tahiti refused to perform their duties; Melville, whose leg was still paining him, was one of them. A fight broke out when one of the mates tried to enforce his orders with his fists. German, who was plainly unfit for command, ordered the ship back to Papeete and then retreated to his cabin.

The unrest on the *Lucy Ann* was not quite a mutiny—there was no extraordinary violence and no attempt to take over the ship—but nonetheless it was a fairly serious matter. Back in Papeete, the British consul, who had authority over Australian ships in the area, took charge of the affair. The "mutineers" were put ashore in the local jail, a thatched hut that was called the calaboose. Herman Melville was among them.

After the *Lucy Ann* sailed in mid-October, the local officials relaxed their guard over the prisoners, most of whom were eventually set free or allowed to wander off. Recognizing that Melville posed no real threat to law and order, the authorities looked the other way when he left the calaboose in the company of John B. Troy, a former surgeon who had served aboard the *Lucy Ann*. Almost before the Australian ship had vanished over the horizon, Melville and Troy were free to explore Tahiti.

One sight that Melville observed closely was the Broom Road, which ran past the calaboose. The road was a monument to missionary fervor in the South Seas, for every yard of its gravel surface had been spread as punishment by someone who had fallen afoul of the local religious police. These judges of public morals rushed to enforce strict laws of behavior in a land that had once known total freedom from petty regulations.

Watching the missionaries, Tahitians, and sailors who passed up and down Broom Road, Melville had a perfect opportunity to study the contrast between two societies: one "civilized" and the other "savage." The conclusions he drew were not very favorable to Western civilization. Although he

Hawaiian rowers in masks. Unlike the majority of nineteenth-century Americans, Melville deplored the destruction of ancient Polynesian cultures by white merchants and missionaries.

had been apprehensive and even frightened among the Taipi, he had also felt a powerful admiration for their carefree, natural way of life, for their unspoiled beauty, and for their traditional culture. He was particularly struck by the fact that they were able to live comfortably off the land with relatively little struggle, and that money and the desire to accumulate material possessions were unknown. Perhaps remembering his father's long fight with bill collectors and creditors, Melville wrote later that the Polynesians' greatest blessing was their "freedom from care and want." At least, that was how the Polynesians had lived before encountering Western values.

In Tahiti, Melville saw the full effect of "civilization" on Polynesia: the introduction of cash that disrupted the traditional island economy; natives who were sick and dying of venereal disease, smallpox, and measles spread by the whites; graceful women forced by missionary prudery to conceal themselves under shapeless dresses; ancient languages, customs, arts, and beliefs being banned so that the Tahitian people would have to adopt the missionaries' alien religion and way of life. As one island group after another fell into the hands of France, Britain, and other Western powers, Melville saw that the Pacific world that had so recently seemed to be an earthly paradise was about to be lost forever. This sense of loss made him both sad and angry, and it colored all his future writings about the Pacific islands.

Melville's only friend during this time was Troy, whose height together with his pale skin and hair earned him the island nickname "The Long Ghost." Troy was a disreputable character—a womanizer and drug abuser who was no longer able to practice surgery—but in some ways Melville found him an entertaining companion. Troy had received a good education and could discuss books and politics; he could also be witty and charming. Lonely and perhaps feeling insecure, Melville formed a close attachment to Troy. They left Tahiti together for the nearby island of Eimeo, which today is known as Mooréa.

Melville and "Dr. Long Ghost" did not spend much time on Eimeo. According to Melville's later account—an account that blurred the line between fact and fiction—they worked for a few days on a potato farm owned by two white farmers, a New Englander and a Londoner, who had helped them get away from Tahiti. During this time they may have hunted wild cattle and pigs in the hills and visited a native village in the island's interior. After a week they left the farm and walked around the small island on the beach—"beachcombing," as this sort of drifting existence was called in the Pacific. Arriving at the village of Papetoi, they spent a few days tak-

ing in the sights: the eighty or so grass huts that housed the
local population; the bamboo-and-thatch palace of Queen
Pomaree, the native ruler of Eimeo; a sugar plantation owned
by a couple of Americans; and a new missionary church that
was the largest building on the island.

As far as Melville was concerned, the most interesting
sight in Papetoi was an American whaler at anchor in the
bay. It was the *Charles and Henry*, which he had seen from a
distance while serving aboard the *Acushnet*. Plagued by the
usual desertions and manpower shortages, Captain John
Coleman of the *Charles and Henry* was recruiting crewmen
among the islands. Melville had no money and did not want
to drift around Eimeo and Tahiti indefinitely—a brief taste of
the beachcomber's life had been enough for him. He
approached Coleman and, after a brief interview, he was
accepted as a member of the crew. It is not known whether
"Dr. Long Ghost" also applied for a position on the *Charles
and Henry* and was turned down, or whether he chose to stay
on the island. Whatever the case, Troy remained behind
when the ship sailed in November of 1842, while Melville
embarked on his third and final whaling venture.

Fortunately, he did not have a bad time aboard the
Charles and Henry. Although the captain was young and inexperienced and months passed without the sight of a single
whale, everyone remained even-tempered and the ship ran
smoothly enough. They sailed through the South Pacific to
the coast of Chile and then, when no whales were to be had,
Coleman set course for the newer whaling grounds in the
North Pacific, off the coast of Japan. On the way to Japan,
they captured a few whales along the Equator and then put in
at the Sandwich Islands—as Hawaii was then called—for
provisions.

The *Charles and Henry* had anchored at the port of Lahaina, on the island of Maui, and there, in May of 1843, Melville took his leave. This time he did not have to desert. He had signed on for a short cruise only and left the ship in good standing, perhaps even with a few dollars in his pocket. He took stock of his prospects, and a few days later he traveled by interisland schooner to Honolulu, on the island of Oahu. As the biggest city in Hawaii, Honolulu offered Melville the best chance of finding a job to support himself while he planned his next move.

5

HOME AGAIN

Once again, Herman Melville's most pressing problem was finding work. His first job in Honolulu was a humble one: he set up pins in a bowling alley. Before long, however, a merchant who planned to open a general store hired Melville as his clerk and bookkeeper. Melville agreed to work for a year in return for lodging, meals, and a salary of $150. The store was not yet ready to open, and with his future provided for—at least one year of it—Melville had a leisurely opportunity to study life and culture in the Hawaiian Islands.

As in Tahiti, he was critical of what he saw. Once again he was convinced that Western civilization was ruining the Islands and the islanders, destroying their centuries-old culture for no good reason. It disturbed him to see the best land taken over by Americans and other whites for their plantations and to see Western-style buildings and roads straggling over the once-lovely land. At the same time native Hawaiians were pushed into menial roles, all in the name of progress and Christianity. In years to come he would write angrily that the Hawaiians "had been civilized into draft horses, and evangelized into beasts of burden."[1]

Melville had a few nervous moments soon after settling in Honolulu. His old ship, the *Acushnet*, came into port, and he had to lie low for fear Captain Pease would learn of his presence and have him arrested as a deserter. But the *Acushnet* spent only one day in Honolulu and left without incident, so Melville was safe. In spite of his dislike of what he called "missionary rule," he apparently intended to remain in Honolulu for the full year of his agreement with the store owner, for he wrote to his mother that he would be in Hawaii until mid-1844. By this time, however, he had been away from home for more than two years, and he longed to see familiar faces and hear familiar voices. His homesickness grew too strong to resist, and by the late summer of 1843 he was thinking of going back to the United States.

Just when he was thinking about returning, Melville was presented with a chance to go home. An American Navy ship, the *United States*, docked in Honolulu. Chatting with sailors from the ship, Melville learned that the *United States* was bound for Boston. He also learned that as a citizen of the United States he could enlist in the Navy, signing up for either three years or the duration of the cruise to Boston. He weighed the decision, balancing his secure position in Honolulu against his desire to see his home and family again. Finally, just two days before the *United States* was scheduled to depart, he made up his mind. He joined the Navy on August 17, 1843.

Having now served aboard four ships—a merchantman and three whalers—Melville considered himself a fairly experienced sea hand. But the Navy, he was soon to discover, did things its own way. No sooner had he learned to clamber into and out of his hammock in the crew's quarters than he was summoned on deck to witness a naval ritual. Two sailors were due to be punished by flogging; one of them was guilty of fighting, the other of smuggling liquor. As usual, the rest of the crew was mustered to watch them receive their punishment. Melville was shocked and sickened by the spectacle.

The culprits were stripped to their waists, tied by their ankles and wrists, and lashed with a whip called the cat-o'-nine-tails. The cat had 9 ends, so a flogging of 12 strokes made 108 bloody welts. The incident was by no means uncommon: Flogging was the standard punishment for most infractions in the Navy, and Melville was to witness 163 floggings during his time on the *United States*. A few years later, in his novel *White-Jacket; or, The World in a Man-of-War*, which was based upon his Navy experience, he vigorously condemned the practice of flogging as unfair and barbaric:

> *Irrespective of incidental considerations, we assert that flogging in the navy is opposed to the essential dignity of man, which no legislator has a right to violate; that it is oppressive, and glaringly unequal in its operations; that it is utterly repugnant to the spirit of our democratic institutions; indeed that it involves a lingering trait of the worst times of a barbarous feudal aristocracy: in a word, we denounce it as religiously, morally, and immutably wrong.*[2]

Melville had other sobering experiences during this homeward cruise. He witnessed five solemn burials at sea, which gave him the chance to absorb many sailors' superstitions about dead bodies and ghosts. And he saw a man fall overboard; the man could not be found, despite a five-hour search by the lifeboats. Finally, because the *United States* was a man-of-war, or battleship, he took part in battle practice, during which he was forced to jump about with a cutlass or haul a heavy, scorchingly hot cannon around the deck. He did not find these exercises thrilling; he hated the thought of war. Most of the time, however, shipboard life was a mind-numbing, dull routine.

The *United States* was the most crowded ship Melville had ever sailed on. Although it was only three-quarters again as large as the *Acushnet*, it carried twenty times as many men. At any given moment, a sailor had only a few square feet of deck or a hammock space to call his own. Whenever he was free from his duties handling sail or cleaning the gun deck, Melville formed the habit of going aloft in the rigging. Perched on the main-royal yard—a swaying spar two hundred feet above the deck—he gazed out across the sea and pondered his recent experiences.

He was not always alone in his hours of reflection. There in the world of air, canvas, and rope, he formed a friendship with Jack Chase, the officer in charge of the mainmast and its rigging. Chase was a thoughtful, honorable, scholarly man whom Melville liked and respected more than anyone else he met in the Pacific. Chase recited poetry in several languages and talked intelligently about literature; he also taught Melville to be proud of good, honest seamanship. Melville later dedicated *White-Jacket* to Jack Chase.

Chase was not the only congenial companion Melville found aboard the *United States*. Along with Chase, he became one of a little group of educated sailors on the ship who frequently met to discuss poetry. Another was Edward Norton, who revealed little about his background and whom Melville regarded as something of a mystery man. Melville recalled long sessions in the night watches when he and Norton "scoured all the prairies of reading; dived into the bosoms of authors, and tore out their hearts."[3] In other words, they discussed books and writers. The two men also went ashore together several times to sightsee when the *United States* was in port. Their paths separated after the ship returned to Boston, but sixteen years later Melville heard from Norton again. His former shipmate had settled down under his real name, Oliver Russ, and had named his son Herman Melville Russ in Melville's honor.

The cruise of the *United States* lasted longer than Melville had expected. Instead of going straight to Boston, the ship toured southern Pacific waters with which Melville was already familiar. It even anchored in Anna Maria Bay at Nuku Hiva, and Melville was able to see the ridge up which he and Toby had scrambled so hopefully many months before. The *United States* also passed Tahiti and Eimeo, giving Melville a chance to look at his old island haunts. Then it was on to South America. The ship docked at Callao, the chief port of Peru, and there Melville heard his first news of a strange sea tragedy that touched him deeply.

A year or so earlier, three men had been hanged for mutiny aboard the Navy ship *Somers*. No one knew exactly what the men had done, but several details made the story unusual. Two of the hanged men were common sailors, but the third was the son of John C. Spencer, the United States secretary of war and thus the official head of the Navy. It was said that he—or perhaps one of the other condemned men— had cried out "God bless the flag!" just before dropping to his death. As the story spread, sailors on every ship cursed the officer on the *Somers* who had condemned the three "muti- neers" to death after a mysterious and secretive court-martial. But Melville was tormented by an additional piece of knowl- edge, which he kept to himself. The officer who had handed down the death sentence was his own cousin, Lieutenant Guert Gansevoort.

Had Guert become a villain? What was the inner truth of the *Somers* affair? Although an official board of inquiry studied the case and decided that Guert had acted within the law, the incident was a subject of rumor and scandal both in the Navy and in government circles in Washington. Guert Gansevoort seldom spoke of it, although he did confide in one relative that he had been pressured into giving the guilty verdict by other ship's officers. Gansevoort never recovered from the effect of the *Somers* hangings; his family saw that his spirit was blighted by the memory. For years, Melville puzzled over this sad drama. Eventually he used it as the basis of his last novel, *Billy Budd*.

The *United States* was in Callao for ten weeks. Upon its departure, Melville took part in one of the greatest spectacles of the age of sail: a man-of-war race. The *United States* and two other warships raced each other out of the harbor. Aboard Melville's vessel the men raced up and down the rigging and piled on every scrap of sail in a frantic attempt to outdistance the competitors, and to their great pride the *United States* won the race. Melville was cheered by this and also by the thought that he was homeward bound at last. He looked forward to sailing south around Cape Horn and then back to New England. But a last-minute order from the Navy sent the *United States* north instead, to Mazatlán, a port on the west coast of Mexico, to pick up a load of silver dollars. The mission took many months, and it was followed by more months of idleness back at Callao while the Navy shuffled officers from ship to ship. Melville had only two days of official free time in almost five months in port, and by the time the *United States* finally lifted anchor for the voyage home he was consumed with boredom and frustration.

Melville had rounded Cape Horn before, on his outward trip to the Pacific. That passage, however, had occurred in the middle of the southern hemisphere's summer. Now he would be facing the Horn in the dead of winter. He had heard tales of the biting winds and bitter frosts that sometimes killed sailors on watch, and he feared that his jacket was not warm enough. So he took needle in hand—like all sailors, he had learned to sew canvas to keep the sails in repair—and made himself a thick, quilted jacket of many layers of white canvas. The jacket was so ungainly and odd looking that it brought some teasing from his shipmates, but it kept him warm during a gale off Cape Horn.

Melville's homeward journey reversed the course of the outward trip he had made nearly four years before. Like the *Acushnet*, the *United States* called briefly at Rio de Janeiro; then it cruised north until, on one memorable day in October of 1844, the ship's cook obtained fresh cod from a Massachusetts fishing boat. When he ate his supper that day, Melville knew that the long journey was almost over.

The next day the *United States* docked in Boston. Melville was discharged from the Navy and promptly threw his white jacket into the Charles River—although he later regretted losing this unique garment and called himself "a great fool" for discarding it. Then he turned his face toward Lansingburgh and home.

Melville found his family's fortunes somewhat less desperate than they had been when he left home. His older brother, Gansevoort, was involved in politics. Allan had become a well-regarded lawyer in New York City. Thomas, the youngest brother, was still at home. However, after hearing Melville describe his adventures, Thomas would soon go to sea and embark on his own Pacific journey. None of Melville's sisters had yet married, and they listened eagerly to tales told by the returned wanderer. Another listener was Elizabeth Shaw, the daughter of Judge Lemuel Shaw, the

Melvilles' family friend, and the favorite companion of Melville's sister Helen. Before long, however, Melville was to think of Elizabeth as more than simply his sister's friend.

Happy though he was to be home, Melville faced the same dilemma that had sent him to sea in the first place: He needed an occupation. But in the weeks after his return, as he held his family and friends spellbound with the story of his sojourn among the cannibal Taipis, he began to get an idea. He believed that if he put his story on paper, he would find a publisher, and the vexing question of his career would be settled at last. He would become a writer.

6

THE SOUTH SEAS NOVELS

For four years, Melville had lived as a man of action, at sea and in distant lands. Now he transformed himself into a man of reflection, a thinker and a teller of tales. Indeed, Melville was to live the rest of his long life as a thinker and a writer rather than a doer. But until the end of his life he continued to draw upon that handful of early, active years for the raw material upon which he set his imagination to work.

As he sat down in his mother's house to write his first book, Melville turned naturally to the one part of his South Seas adventure about which everyone was most curious: his stay "among the cannibals." The story was his own, certainly, but in writing *Typee: A Peep at Polynesian Life* Melville established a habit that he would follow throughout his career. He used his own experiences as the skeleton of the book and then fleshed it out with creative imagination and diligent research. In *Typee*, he wrote about his escape with Toby from a whaling vessel (which he called the *Dolly* rather than the *Acushnet*), their mistaken descent into the valley of the cannibals, the things they saw and did while living with the Taipis, and their separate departures from the valley—departures that Melville presented as desperate escapes from the gruesome fate of the long pig. He took some liberties with the truth. Among other things, he lengthened his stay in the valley from four weeks to four months. He also made the Polynesian girl Fayaway into a major romantic character, whatever her role in real life may have been.

Melville knew that readers of his time would expect more from a book about the South Seas than simply a rousing adventure. In the mid-nineteenth century, no book set in a remote corner of the earth was complete without colorful, informative details about local tribes, customs, and natural history, and Melville would be expected to provide plenty of this type of information. Of course, everything he said was supposed to be based on his own observation, but in reality Melville was always more interested in ideas and feelings than in the concrete details of sights and sounds. He simply had not absorbed enough background information and local color to fill a book. His answer was to turn to other books. He joined his brothers Gansevoort and Allan in New York City and studied Polynesia in the city's library, consulting books about the Pacific that had been published in the previous decades. These included *Voyages Around the World*, by Edmund Fanning, a New England sea captain, and David Porter's *Journal of a Cruise Made to the Pacific Ocean in the Frigate Essex*. Most interesting of his research sources, however, was Charles S. Stuart's *A Visit to the South Seas*, for this was an account of the voyage during which Melville's cousin Thomas had visited the Marquesas Islands. Melville borrowed many of his descriptions of Taipi life and customs from these volumes. One reason he had to exaggerate the length of his stay with the Taipis, in fact, was so that Tommo, as he called the book's narrator, would have enough time in the valley to witness all the ceremonies, battles, and other events that he wanted to describe.

The result of Melville's labors was a unique blend of fact and fiction. Today *Typee* is regarded as a novel—that is, a fictional narrative—although it is considered an autobiographical novel because it closely follows events in its author's life. Yet Melville presented it as a straightforward travel book, an unvarnished account of his experiences and of Polynesian life. With Gansevoort's help, he found a publisher: John Murray of London, who specialized in factual books about travel and history. *Typee* was published in London in February of 1846 and in the United States about a month later. When some critics suggested that the book was fiction, not fact, Murray was upset, and he demanded proof from Melville that the young author had actually been in the South Seas.

Murray's demand placed Melville in an awkward position. Although Melville could prove that he had been in the Pacific, he had no proof that he had lived among the cannibals, and he knew that he had exaggerated or even made up some parts of his story. Luckily for Melville, timely support came from a surprise ally. Richard Tobias Greene, his old shipmate on the *Acushnet* and fellow deserter, stepped forward. He had become a sign painter in Buffalo, New York, and he wrote to a newspaper calling himself "the true and veritable Toby" and claimed that the parts of *Typee* in which he appeared were true. Melville gratefully visited Tobias Greene and added a chapter called "The Story of Toby" to the next edition of the book.

Despite some carping over its accuracy, *Typee* was well liked by most critics and readers on both sides of the Atlantic Ocean. Europeans and Americans still knew very little about the Pacific world, and fascinated readers took the story to their hearts. The book's American publisher even said that he found it as interesting as *Robinson Crusoe*, that classic of exotic adventure. This was high praise indeed. Among the reviewers who spoke favorably of *Typee* were two men who now rank with Melville among the towering figures of nineteenth-century American literature: Nathaniel Hawthorne and Walt Whitman.

One group of readers, however, was less enthusiastic. Melville's views about the South Seas were clear in *Typee*, and his criticisms of "the rape of the islands" by missionaries and colonialists roused the anger of missionary societies and their earnest supporters. They condemned *Typee* and its author as immoral. At the insistence of his American editor, Evert A. Duyckinck, Melville removed the unflattering references to missionaries from the American edition of the book. Duyckinck and Melville were to become friends, but their friendship was later strained by their differing points of view. Duyckinck was conventional, socially correct, and a bit stuffy, while Melville remained a free thinker who was less concerned with what people thought of him than with exploring the world of ideas.

During the first months of *Typee*'s success, Melville was busy with family matters. Gansevoort Melville, whose health had never been strong, died suddenly in London, and Melville returned to the family home in Lansingburgh to mourn with his mother. He also tried to convince sixteen-year-old Thomas, his youngest brother, not to go off to sea, but he failed, and Thomas made a career in the Navy. Melville also paid a visit to the Boston home of Judge Lemuel Shaw to give the judge an autographed copy of *Typee*, for he had dedicated the book to Shaw. The presence of Elizabeth Shaw certainly helped draw the young author to Boston.

Melville was filled with confidence and relief at the suc-

*Portraitist Asa Twitchell captured Melville around 1847,
the year of his marriage.*

cess of his first book. He believed that he had at last found his
role in life—something he enjoyed that would also allow him
to make a living. In this state of mind, he settled down in
Lansingburgh to work on a second book. Like *Typee*, it was to
be closely based on his own adventures. He called it *Omoo*,
and it took up the story of his wanderings through the Pacific
Islands where *Typee* left off.

The first third of *Omoo* covers Melville's time on the Australian whaler, the *Lucy Ann* (called the *Julia* in the book),

ending with the mutiny aboard that ship. Melville then wrote about his imprisonment in the calaboose in Tahiti, his friendship with Dr. Long Ghost, and his visit to the island of Eimeo. At the book's end, the hero is ready to leave Eimeo on another whaling voyage. This trip corresponds to Melville's departure on the *Charles and Henry*. As in *Typee*, Melville made no sharp distinction between fact and fiction. He exaggerated the drama of events and his own role in them, making the mutiny sound more serious and his imprisonment more severe than they really were. As Leon Howard pointed out in his 1951 biography, Melville was becoming too good a "yarn spinner" to let his story suffer just because the raw material of his experience was not as exciting as it could be. Nevertheless, many literary scholars believe that *Omoo* comes closest of all of Melville's books to true autobiography, presenting events almost as they happened.

In addition to a bit of exaggeration, Melville drew heavily upon books such as *Polynesian Researches* for descriptions of Tahitian village life. Ironically, the author of *Polynesian Researches*, William Ellis, was a missionary, but Melville's attack on the missionaries was even harsher in *Omoo* than in *Typee*. Although Melville did agree to take some of his strongest antimissionary remarks out of the manuscript, the Wiley and Putnam publishing firm, which had produced *Typee* in the United States, felt that the book might be too controversial. Wiley and Putnam decided not to buy *Omoo*, which was published by Harper and Brothers in 1847 instead.

Omoo—the title means "the rover" or "the wanderer"— received the expected thrashing from the missionaries, but it proved to be a major hit with the public. It contained more humor than *Typee*, reminding some readers of the comic novels of British author Charles Dickens, the most beloved writer of the age. *Omoo* may have been the most widely read of Herman Melville's books during his lifetime. He reached the peak of his popularity with this book, only his second. For the rest of his career, he would try again and again to recapture that early popular success, but in vain.

As he basked in the success of *Omoo*, Melville foresaw a rosy future for himself. He knew, however, that authorship was an uncertain profession. It did not guarantee steady financial security, and security was always important to Melville. The background of his family's constant money troubles gave him a perpetual dread of financial failure. At this time, too, Melville had a special reason for seeking financial security. He was thinking of getting married to Elizabeth Shaw. Elizabeth returned his affection, and they became engaged. Melville applied for a job as a clerk in the United States Treasury Department, believing that a position in a government office would offer security and still give him time to write. But just as his earlier hope of working on the Erie Canal had been doomed to disappointment, he failed to get the job. Melville was hurt and angry, feeling that he and his family deserved some recognition and favor from the government. After all, as he often reminded himself and others, the Melvilles *and* the Gansevoorts were people of importance who had helped win the American Revolution.

Disappointed though he was over his failure to obtain a civil service job, Melville kept busy during the summer of 1847. Deciding that his only immediate prospect of earning a living was to keep writing, he started a third book. Together with his brother Allan, he bought a house in New York City. Allan was getting married, too, and the brothers planned to share the house. Melville also spent some time in Lansingburgh, visiting his mother and working in her garden, before going to Boston for the round of parties and other social events that preceded his wedding on August 4, 1847. In later years, Melville's clearest memory of his wedding day was of taking a walk and finding a four-leaf clover, which he preserved as a token of good fortune for the marriage.

The newlyweds set off on a honeymoon journey by train, stagecoach, and boat through New Hampshire and part of Canada. They stayed in Montreal and Quebec, determinedly sightseeing despite steady rain, and returned through the scenic mountains of Vermont. Then they settled down with Allan and his new wife at their home at 103 Fourth Avenue, in the part of lower New York City that is called Greenwich Village. Evert Duyckinck, Melville's editor and new friend, was a near neighbor. Duyckinck and his brother started a literary magazine, and they invited Melville to write occasional articles and reviews. These did not produce any significant income for their author, but they gave him useful writing experience and established him as an active member of the literary community.

The Melvilles' house in New York was large but crowded. In addition to the two newly married couples, Melville's mother, Maria, moved in, along with his four unmarried sisters. Melville and Elizabeth had two rooms to themselves, but the rest of the house bustled with the activities of other family members. Melville formed the habit of leaving the house in the evenings to spend a restful hour or two with Duyckinck or other literary friends in the neighborhood, but Elizabeth was not so fortunate. Perhaps she secretly wished that she and Melville could have a small house of their own—not an unreasonable wish for a young bride. She wrote to her parents that Maria Melville dominated the household and that she was "sick and tired" of the situation. Yet she smiled and hid her dissatisfaction from her husband, for she did not want to make him unhappy while he was working so hard on his new book.

Elizabeth Shaw Melville in 1847. Although she helped Melville in his work, writing out the final drafts of some of his books to spare his eyesight, she urged him for years to get a steady job.

Melville had settled into a working routine that he was to follow, with few changes, for many years. After breakfast with the whole family, he took a walk while Elizabeth straightened his room. On his return, he wrote in uninterrupted solitude for four hours. He and Elizabeth lunched with the family and took a walk together before Melville returned to his labors for another two hours. After dinner he might call on friends, or scan the newspapers in a public reading room, although he was beginning to have trouble with his eyesight and could do very little reading or writing by candlelight. Later the family generally gathered in the communal parlor for games or conversation until everyone went to bed at ten. It was a highly structured life. Elizabeth—who had nothing to do all day but pay social calls and tidy her room—may have chafed at the dull routine, but Melville found it productive.

He had done his research for *Typee* in the libraries of New York, but as soon as he sold his first book he began a lifelong habit of purchasing the books he needed for research. Melville's Greenwich Village neighborhood was filled with bookstores, of which only a few remain today. He loved prowling through these stores, and whenever he traveled he sought out bookstalls and musty secondhand bookstores. He also bought a great many books from his various publishers, charging the purchase price against the amount that the publisher owed him in royalties on the sales of his own books. This system was convenient—perhaps too convenient. It allowed Melville to consume a substantial share of his earnings in the form of books, not cash income. As his career continued, he bought so many books, and some of his own sold so poorly, that much of the time he owed money to his publishers instead of the other way around.

But for Melville, reading was an important part of writing. It not only provided him with factual information but also stimulated his imagination, as did his conversations about politics, philosophy, and other subjects with his new friends. Like the hours he had once spent discussing poetry with Jack Chase and Edward Norton aboard the *United States*, these gatherings gave Melville the welcome and exciting feeling that he was embarked on an intellectual adventure, that he was growing mentally. He later wrote to Nathaniel Hawthorne: "Until I was twenty-five I had no development at all. From my twenty-fifth year I date my life. Three weeks have scarcely passed, at any time between then and now, that I have not unfolded within myself."[1] Melville had turned twenty-five just after *Typee* was published, and now, settled into a new life with a new book on the way, he thrilled to the sense of inner growth just as he had once thrilled to the roar of a storm in the rigging.

As always when he was writing a book, Melville's reading was organized around the subject of his work. He planned to turn for the third time to his Pacific experiences, taking up the story at the point where he left Eimeo on the *Charles and Henry*. In preparation, he read a book about whaling, and he also studied British naturalist Charles Darwin's account of his 1831–36 voyage around the world in the ship *Beagle* (like Melville, Darwin had been fascinated by the Galápagos Islands). A decade or so later, Darwin was to shake up the scientific and religious communities with his theory of evolution. But in the late 1840s Melville was interested only in picturesque anecdotes and scientific details he could borrow from Darwin to flavor his own book.

One of Melville's other book purchases at this time is especially interesting in light of his later masterpiece, *Moby-Dick*. He bought and read a six-volume account by Charles Wilkes of an American exploring expedition in the South Pacific Ocean in the years 1838–42. Wilkes had commanded the expedition, which was plagued with disputes, large-scale desertions, and the loss of several ships. Controversy surrounded Wilkes, who had run the expedition in a strict and eccentric manner; there were even rumors that he was mad. Some modern critics feel that Ahab, the secretive, tyrannical, obsessed captain in *Moby-Dick*, may be based in part on Wilkes. But the narrative of the Wilkes expedition provided Melville with much more than hints of character. It contained useful maps of the Pacific; engravings of plants, fish, and animals; and descriptions of the native peoples of New Zealand and other places that Melville himself had not visited. He certainly used much of this material in *Moby-Dick*, but that book was still several years away. The book he was now writing was to be called *Mardi and a Voyage Thither*.

It started as a tale of travel and adventure in the vein of *Typee* and *Omoo*, with its narrator aboard a whaler bound for the Japan seas. Soon after the beginning of the story, the young hero and a companion desert their ship in a small boat and make a suspenseful journey in search of land. Up to this point, *Mardi* is a vigorous, exciting maritime adventure, but about one-quarter of the way through the book, the tone suddenly changes. From a swashbuckling saga, the book becomes a philosophical allegory—that is, a story in which people, places, and objects are not portrayed realistically but are supposed to represent certain qualities, virtues, vices, or aspects of life. In an allegory, the characters' actions embody moral or intellectual lessons.

Instead of arriving in Tahiti, or Hawaii, or some other place that exists in the real world, Melville's hero lands in Mardi, an imaginary island kingdom situated on the equator. There he is given the name Taji and joins a group of characters who represent various concepts. The king, Media, stands for the mind; Yoomy, a dreamy, long-haired fellow, represents poetry; the talkative Babbalanja symbolizes philosophy, and so on. Taji also meets two women. Hautia is a cruel and seductive temptress, while Yillah represents everything that is true, pure, and beautiful. Taji falls in love with Yillah and pursues her through a series of fantastic islands, in each of which Melville satirizes or examines a different feature of society. The island of Vivenza, for example, is clearly meant to refer to the United States, and Melville paints a scornful picture of greedy politicians. He also criticizes slavery, which he hated. Taji searches in Vivenza and many other places for Yillah, but he does not find her. Truth, Melville seems to be saying, cannot be found among the countries of this world. Finally Taji dies, claiming that he is going to seek Yillah in the next world.

Mardi had somehow changed course drastically while Melville was writing it. What had started as a simple travel tale had taken on unexpected dimensions of fantasy, romance, satire, and philosophy. Although Melville does not seem to have planned the change, he apparently enjoyed it. He clearly relished the play of ideas in the allegorical part of the book, and he had fun satirizing the pompous people and institutions of civilized life. Some critics have suggested that *Mardi* was an attempt by Melville to make his writing more attractive to women. Melville never spoke of his intentions for *Mardi*, so we do not know if this theory is correct. One thing we do know is that Elizabeth Melville was very fond of a literary device called floral symbolism that was popular in the nineteenth century. Floral symbolism used various flowers to represent certain specific meanings—roses meant sexual love, for example, while lilies meant death. Melville used a very elaborate form of floral symbolism throughout *Mardi*, apparently to please Elizabeth, for it does not appear in his other work.

Whatever his reasons for departing from his original plan for the book, Melville was confident that it would be a hit with the public. He needed another successful, moneymaking book, for he and Elizabeth had started a family. Their first child, a boy whom they named Malcolm, was born in February of 1849, after Melville had finished writing his third book but before it was published. But, although Melville thought that *Mardi* would be more universally popular than either *Typee* or *Omoo*, he did recognize that it was a most unusual type of book.

In the text of the book, he described Lombardo, an

ancient Mardian writer, in words that might have applied to himself while writing *Mardi*: "When Lombardo set about his work, he knew not what it would become. He did not build himself in with plans; he wrote right on; and in so doing, he got deeper and deeper into himself."[2] His description of Lombardo's masterpiece is a good description of *Mardi* itself:

> *It is wild, unconnected, nothing but episodes; valleys and hills; rivers, digressing from plains; vines, roving all over; boulders and diamonds; flowers and thistles; forests and thickets; and, here and there, fens and moors.*[3]

In the preface he wrote for *Mardi*, Melville modestly alerted his readers to expect something different. He joked that those who thought he had made up his earlier, "true" stories might now think that his new fable was true, and that Mardi really existed:

> *Having published two narratives of voyages in the Pacific, which, in many quarters, were received with incredulity, the thought occurred to me of indeed writing a romance of Polynesian adventure, and publishing it as such; to see whether the fiction might not, possibly, be received for a verity: in some degree the reverse of my previous experience.*[4]

Melville had high hopes for *Mardi*, but the book's reception was a crushing blow to those hopes. *Mardi* puzzled and frustrated both book reviewers and readers; they did not know what to make of it. Some people liked the fantasy and allegory parts of the book, and others liked the adventure part, but no one liked the combination.

The *Boston Post* called the book "not only tedious but unreadable," and a leading magazine warned that of the hundred people who might pick up the book because they remembered *Typee*, only one would read it all the way through. The reviewers in England were equally discouraging. A magazine issued by Melville's own publisher could find nothing better to say about *Mardi* than that it was a book "which the reader will probably like very much or detest altogether." Judging from the sales figures, few readers liked *Mardi* very much, and most simply ignored it. Several critics warned Melville to return to the more easily understandable style of *Typee* and *Omoo* if he wanted to keep any readers at all.

As soon as *Mardi* was published, Melville realized that he was not going to make any money from it. He found himself in the position he loathed: short of funds, with bills to pay. Elizabeth had a small income given to her by her father, but Melville still needed to earn some money quickly. The only thing he could think of was to write another book at once. This time, he decided rather grimly, he would not be lured down any flowery paths of intellectual or philosophical speculation, no matter how tempting they seemed to him. He would give the public what it wanted, no more and no less. By May of 1849 he was at work. The book was finished by the end of June.

Typee and *Omoo* had been well received and, more important, they had earned Melville at least a modest income. For his fourth book, Melville returned to the formula that had worked in those two earlier books. He told the story of a young man's adventures at sea and out in the world, based on his own experiences but seasoned with a little extra drama and heightened color. The result was *Redburn: His First Voyage*, a book that Melville considered a potboiler (a term used by artists and writers for inferior works that are produced just to please the public and make money). Complaining of bills and creditors, the harassed author wrote to his friend Duyckinck:

*When a poor devil writes with duns all round him, and
looking over the back of his chair—and perching on his pen
and diving in his inkstand—like the devils about St.
Anthony—what can you expect of that poor devil?—
What but a beggarly "Redburn!"*[5]

Redburn was based on Melville's summer voyage to Liverpool and back in 1839 aboard the merchantman *St. Lawrence*.
Melville dedicated this tale of a boy's first voyage to his
brother Thomas, who was away on a voyage to China.
Although to Melville *Redburn* was always a "beggarly" potboiler, in fact it is a worthy book. The story is dramatically
told, with a slow buildup of tension to a gruesome (and
entirely fictitious) climax on the homeward voyage. Melville's
language is strong, controlled, and vivid, and his descriptions
of Liverpool's squalid slums are deeply moving. The characters in *Redburn* seem more like flesh-and-blood people than
any Melville had yet created.

Melville also emphasized the element of social criticism
in *Redburn*. One of the book's themes was the condition of
the urban poor. Another was immigration. During the 1840s,
thousands of people from England, Ireland, and Europe tried
to escape poverty and despair by moving to the United
States. Many Americans worried about this flood of immigrants, claiming that the country should close its doors. In
Redburn, Melville described a crowd of anxious immigrants
crammed into the ship, waiting for their first sight of America. Writing of what he called "that agitated national topic,
as to whether such multitudes of foreign poor should be
landed on our American shores," Melville showed a tolerant,
humanitarian attitude.[6] He believed that all people are part
of one global family, and he wrote: "For the whole world is
the patrimony of the whole world; there is no telling who

does not own a stone in the Great Wall of China."[7]

Deploring the inhumanity and brutality that so-called civilized people so often showed toward one another, Melville commented: "We talk of the Turks, and abhor the cannibals, but may not some of *them* go to heaven, before some of *us*? We may have civilized bodies and yet barbarous souls."[8] These and other reflections gave *Redburn* a depth of meaning beyond that of a mere potboiler. If Melville had overestimated the value of *Mardi*, in *Redburn* he had written a better book than he knew.

7

WHITE-JACKET AND A NEW FRIEND

*R*edburn was published in the early autumn of 1849, half a year after the publication of *Mardi*. The book won favorable reviews and achieved some popularity, but even before it was published Melville had known that however big a hit he made with *Redburn*, he would barely earn enough from it to settle his debts to his publishers. To get ahead, he would have to produce another book right away. He worked in feverish haste through the summer, while *Redburn* was being prepared for the press. By September he had finished writing his fifth book in four years. He considered it his second potboiler.

The new book was called *White-Jacket; or, The World in a Man-of-War*. It is an account of a voyage on a Navy man-of-war called the *Neversink*, loosely based on Melville's stint in the Navy and his 14-month cruise in the *United States*. The book's hero, White-Jacket, is a solitary, thoughtful young sailor who shields himself from the cold with a homemade white jacket like the one Melville had made for himself on that voyage. Throughout the book, White-Jacket represents the point of view of a naive innocent, someone not yet hardened to the ways of the world or to cruelty. The whiteness of his jacket is a symbol of his spiritual purity and innocence.

Of all the novels based on the events of Melville's own life, however, *White-Jacket* is the least strictly autobiographical. It contains many incidents that did not really happen to Melville: The sailors run out of liquor and start drinking perfume instead; the ship's crew celebrates the Fourth of July in the waters off Cape Horn; White-Jacket narrowly escapes being flogged; the sadistic ship's surgeon performs an amputation; and the crew lands in Brazil and is reviewed by the emperor of that country.

Some of these events were taken from contemporary books such as *Life in a Man-of-War*, by James Mercier, or *Tales of the Ocean and Forecastle*, by S. S. Sleeper. Melville bought these volumes and kept them at hand as a source of incidents for his story. Many events that Melville described vividly— such as the hero's terrifying fall from the masthead into the sea—were long thought by literary critics to be his own experiences, until the old logbooks of the *United States* were carefully searched. When no mention of this incident and others was found, scholars were able to trace them to books he had read.

Admittedly, part of *White-Jacket*'s subject matter was borrowed. But the novel, like *Redburn*, was still a better book than its author gave it credit for being. Although it does not rank as a masterpiece among Melville's works, it was superior to the run-of-the-mill sea stories that were published by the score during the nineteenth century. As in *Redburn*, Melville used the events and characters of the voyage, filtered through the eyes and mind of a young, innocent observer, to point up truths about human life. He criticized the hypocrisy of the ship's chaplain, who was supposed to serve Christ but who shared the bounty money that was paid out when the *Neversink* destroyed enemy ships "full of human beings." He protested against the brutality of naval practices such as flogging, and in the contrast between the drunken, incompetent captain and the noble, capable Jack Chase, captain of the foretop, he raised such questions as: What is true leadership? How should people in authority behave? All in all, the book expressed Melville's belief that military life was mindless and degrading, "a system of cruel cogs and wheels, systematically grinding up in one common hopper all that might minister to the moral well-being of the crew."[1]

By the time he wrote *White-Jacket*, Melville had mastered the use of language. The book contains none of the awkward sentences that occasionally mar *Typee*, his first effort. *White-Jacket* closes with a burst of poetic inspiration in which Melville compares the frigate *Neversink* to the world and each life to a mysterious voyage:

As a man-of-war that sails through the sea, so this earth that sails through the air. We mortals are all on board a fast-sailing, never-sinking world-frigate, of which God was the shipwright; and she is but one craft in a Milky-Way fleet, of which God is the Lord High Admiral. The port we sail from is forever astern. And though far out of sight of land, for ages and ages we continue to sail with sealed orders, and our last destination remains a secret to ourselves and our officers; yet our final haven was predestined ere we slipped from the docks at Creation.

Thus sailing with sealed orders, we ourselves are the repositories of the secret packet, whose mysterious contents we long to learn. There are no mysteries out of ourselves.[2]

On the voyage of life, Melville states, all people are ship-mates and must learn to care for one another, to treat one another with compassion rather than indifference or violence:

Oh, ship-mates and world-mates, all round! we the people suffer many abuses. Our gun-deck is full of complaints. In vain from Lieutenants do we appeal to the Captain; in vain—while we board our world-frigate—to the indefinite Navy Commissioners so far aloft. Yet the worst of our evils we blindly inflict upon ourselves; our officers cannot remove them, even if they would. From the last ills no being can save another; therein each man must be his own saviour. For the rest, whatever befall us, let us never train our murderous guns inboard; let us not mutiny with bloody pikes in our hands.[3]

Melville's American publisher, Harper and Brothers, bought *White-Jacket* but agreed not to issue it until Melville could go to England and sell the book there as well, for Melville expected to get more money from an English publisher if the book had not yet appeared in the United States. He set out from New York for London in October of 1849 aboard the *Southampton*. It was Melville's sixth voyage by ship, and the first he had boarded as a passenger.

The voyage was enjoyable. At last, after a period of exhausting activity during which he had written three books without a break, Melville had a chance to relax. He did not even feel like reading, much less writing. On the first day at sea, he amazed his fellow passengers by climbing coolly to the top of the mainmast to look at the wide, featureless sea horizon, and throughout the trip he occasionally scampered into the rigging. He had the additional pleasure of seeing a passenger reading *Omoo* in her deck chair and feeling the thrill of authorship.

Melville forced himself to do a little writing during the trip. He kept a journal. Writing in a journal, or diary, was an almost universal practice among authors, but Melville had never taken up the habit. He knew, however, that a journal could save him much of the trouble and expense of researching his books. He told himself that if he had had the good sense to keep a journal in the Pacific, he would not have had to read so many other books to find material for his first two novels. (Melville did not seem to wonder whether he would have been able to keep a journal through such escapades as mountain climbing on Nuku Hiva, imprisonment on Tahiti, or beachcombing on Eimeo. He knew very well that many intrepid nineteenth-century travelers had staunchly managed to produce thousands of pages of journal entries in the most adverse conditions, from the Amazon rain forest to the Arctic Circle. Many travel books of the time featured scenes of shipwrecks or other disasters in which the author said something along the lines of "I had only time to snatch up my precious journal and run.")

According to Melville's journal, the most satisfying feature of the voyage on the *Southampton* was the new friendships he formed with two passengers: a German scholar named George Adler, with whom he strolled the deck and discussed philosophy and the meaning of life, and an American physician named Franklin Taylor, with whom he made plans for an ambitious excursion to Turkey and Egypt (the plans fell through, however, because neither man had enough money to make the trip). Upon arriving in London, the three men took rooms in the same hotel and then saw the sights and attended concerts and plays together.

Melville's first order of business was to see whether *Red-*

burn had yet been published in England. He was reassured by the sight of it in a bookstore, where he indignantly refused the owner's attempts to sell him a copy of the book. Then he tracked down the English reviews, which were fairly good. One magazine gave *Redburn* a particularly long, earnest review, and Melville wrote in his journal that he was surprised the editor would "waste so many pages upon a thing which I, the author, know to be trash, and wrote it to buy some tobacco with."[4]

Next Melville called upon several British publishers. To his great relief—for he was almost completely penniless—he was given a check for the British edition of *Redburn*. Later he managed to sell *White-Jacket* for twice as much as he had received for *Redburn*. The business part of his trip had been successful, he wrote jubilantly in his journal, scrawling, "Hurrah and three cheers!"[5]

Melville had more on his mind than business, however. He also wanted to gather material for a new book. He was thinking of writing a novel based not on his own experience but on the story of Israel Potter, an American soldier who had fought in the Revolutionary War. Potter had been captured by the British and spent fifty years living in exile in London. Determined to collect details that he could use in his book, Melville roamed the London streets, soaking up impressions. Like Charles Dickens, probably the most popular author of the time, Melville saw much that was striking and appalling in the London of the mid-nineteenth century. Describing the fog, grime, and teeming tenements of the city slums, Melville was reminded of hell. On one occasion he witnessed a banquet hosted by the mayor. Then, behind the building, he watched beggars fighting over scraps thrown from the banquet table. He even went to see a public hanging and reported that the brutish mob that gathered for the spectacle

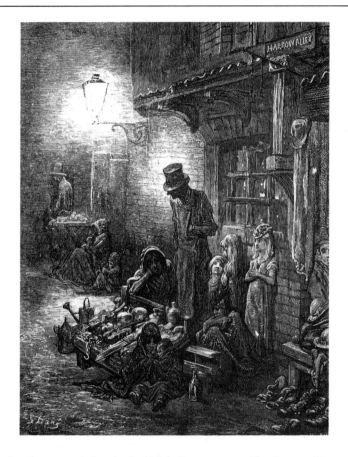

The London poverty that shocked Melville, as engraved by Gustave Doré, one of the leading illustrators of the late nineteenth century.

was a more "wonderful, horrible, and unspeakable scene" than the execution itself.

Despite limited funds and growing homesickness, Melville was determined to see a bit of Europe while he had the chance. He made a fifteen-day trip to Paris, Brussels, and Cologne, staying in cheap lodging houses and cramming his days with as many museums, theaters, and other sights as he could manage. Upon returning to London in mid-December, he found to his astonishment that he had been invited to visit the Duke of Rutland's country house in January.

The invitation posed a dilemma. Melville was deeply flattered by the attention from a member of the nobility, and he was also intensely curious about the duke's castle and family. He realized that he might never again have the chance to observe the English aristocracy on its home ground. "If I do not go, I am confident that hereafter I will upbraid myself for neglecting such an opportunity of procuring 'material.' And Allan and others will account me a ninny," he confided anxiously to his journal.[6] But the duke's invitation was nearly a month away, and Melville was desperately eager to be home with his wife and child. Homesickness won out over curiosity, and Melville regretfully turned down the invitation and booked passage home. To save money, he returned on a sailing ship and not on the faster but more expensive steamship. He arrived in New York in February of 1850 loaded down with books and maps he had unearthed in the bookshops of London and Paris.

Back at home, Melville was happy to see good reviews of his two new books. One reviewer called Melville "the most captivating of ocean authors." *Redburn* was selling well, and *White-Jacket* promised to do even better. (Both books, in fact, sold out their entire first edition of four thousand copies within a few months, and immediately went into second editions.) *Typee* and *Omoo* were still in print. Sales of the earlier books actually picked up when *Redburn* and *White-Jacket* appeared. Although Melville privately felt that he had capitulated by writing books for popular appeal alone, at least he could console himself with the belief that his income was improving. Melville may not have realized that only a small handful of top-selling authors could count on writing as their sole source of income. Most writers also received money from jobs, investments, or their families. But Melville believed he could support his family by writing alone. He felt so confident of his financial security that he decided to move out of the New York City house he shared with his brother and sister-in-law and their growing family, his mother, and his four sisters. Elizabeth was particularly eager to get out of the city because she had developed severe allergies that were most troublesome in urban summer weather.

Melville, too, may have desired more peace and quiet than he was ever likely to get in the Fourth Avenue house. His thoughts turned to Pittsfield, Massachusetts, where during his boyhood he had enjoyed summers on his uncle Thomas's farm nestled among the Berkshire Mountains. He rented the old Melville household in Pittsfield for the summer and moved his wife and son there in July 1850.

That summer was a joyous time for Melville. Relieved—at least for the moment—of money worries, he threw himself into a round of parties and excursions with his Pittsfield neighbors and visiting friends from New York. For several months, his social life was the busiest it was ever to be. The Duyckincks came from New York to stay for a while, as did Allan Melville and his wife. Melville hosted a festive house party that included a picnic on a peak called Monument Mountain. Local residents and summer visitors made up the picnic party, and among them were a number of literary figures: Melville and the Duyckincks, the essayist and poet Oliver Wendell Holmes, a publisher named James T. Fields, and one of Fields's authors, Nathaniel Hawthorne, who lived in the nearby town of Lenox and had just published what was to become his best-known novel, *The Scarlet Letter* (1850).

The Monument Mountain trip was a memorable occasion. Melville, who was generally quiet in company, became unusually lively. When he spotted a projecting spur of rock

that looked like the bowsprit of a ship, he climbed out to its
end and pretended to be hauling on a ship's rigging, to the
amusement of his friends. Near the summit of the mountain,
the climbers were caught by a sudden thunderstorm. They
took shelter in a shallow cave, and Holmes passed around
champagne in a silver cup.

According to literary legend, Melville and Hawthorne
talked about philosophy and literature while they were waiting for the rain to stop, and became fast friends. Whatever
the truth of this story, the two men certainly did become
friends, and the friendship meant a great deal to Melville.
Hawthorne was older—forty-six to Melville's thirty-one —
and better established as a writer. To Melville he seemed not
only a friend but also a guide and mentor. Melville immediately wrote a praiseful review of Hawthorne's work for the
Duyckincks' literary magazine, although he did not sign the
review and Hawthorne did not know that Melville was its
author. Hawthorne, for his part, spoke favorably of some of
Melville's books and had a high opinion of his young friend's
mind.

Melville had such a good time in Pittsfield that summer
that he decided to move his family there permanently. With
the help of a large loan from his father-in-law, he bought a
farm next to Thomas Melville's former home. It had 160
acres of land and a view of Mount Greylock. He named his
new estate Arrowhead, after an Indian arrowhead that he
found in one of his fields.

8

THE "WHALE"

If Melville and Elizabeth had looked forward to having their own home at last, they were doubtless dismayed when Melville's mother, the domineering Maria Melville, announced that she and her four daughters would also be moving to Arrowhead. This naturally made the process of getting settled into the new house much more tense and complicated. By October, however, the bustle of moving had subsided somewhat, the corn and pumpkins on the new farm had been harvested, wood had been chopped for the winter, and Melville was free to return to his writing.

He had already begun a new book. In fact, Melville had started writing soon after his return from England in February. In high spirits over the good reception of *Redburn* and *White-Jacket*, he abandoned—for the time being—the story of Israel Potter, the American soldier. He decided instead to draw upon the only piece of his own seafaring life that he had not yet made into a book: whaling. He wrote to his British publisher that he planned to write a "romance of adventure founded upon certain wild legends of the Southern Sperm

Arrowhead, the Massachusetts farm that was Melville's country sanctuary, is now a Melville memorial.

Whale Fisheries, and illustrated by the author's own personal experience, of two years or more, as a harpooner."[1]

Melville had indeed served on three whaleships, but it is by no means certain that he ever really harpooned a whale. He had, however, studied all aspects of the whaling life and experienced many of them firsthand. And he had absorbed his shipmates' tales, the "wild legends" of Mocha Dick, the white whale, and the whale attack that sank the *Essex*. These and other stories, memories, and scraps of knowledge swirled in his head as he began writing the book that he was to call *Moby-Dick; or The Whale* (Melville never explained why he put a hyphen in the book's title but not in the whale's name when it appeared in the text).

In writing *Moby-Dick*, Melville followed his usual custom of fleshing out his narrative with incidents, facts, and colorful details from other books. As early as April he had begun ordering books about whales and the whaling industry to supplement his own knowledge and experience. But whaling books were not the only reading that influenced Melville while he was writing *Moby-Dick*. Many other literary sources helped shape his book. In fact, in 1849 and 1850 Melville discovered literature. He had never been a particularly passionate reader, but now he plunged joyously into the works of poets, novelists, and essayists past and present. He was in a constant state of excitement about what he was reading and about the pleasures of literature.

One important influence upon his own literary style was William Shakespeare. After seeing the famous actress Fanny Kemble perform in Shakespeare's play *Macbeth* in 1849, Melville had begun enthusiastically reading Shakespeare's works. He called himself a "dolt and ass" for not having read the great dramatist earlier. Melville's views about Shakespeare echoed those of the eighteenth- and nineteenth-century critics who felt that the dramatist's best creations were his tragic heroes. Melville agreed with Samuel Taylor Coleridge, the British poet and critic, who had declared in 1813 that Shakespeare's most impressive characters were "diseased or mutilated" in some way, physically or psychologically. Each hero had a fatal flaw that brought about his downfall.

The influence of Shakespeare is also clear in the language and structure of *Moby-Dick*. The novel has many of the qualities of drama. Certain chapters are written in the form of scenes in a play, and Ahab and other characters often express themselves in poetic speeches similar to those uttered by Shakespeare's characters, rather than in the colorful but simple language that seamen would ordinarily use.

Melville was also influenced by the thinking of Thomas Carlyle, a British man of letters who explored the idea of heroism in his book *On Heroes, Hero-Worship, and the Heroic*

in History (1841). To Carlyle, a person achieved heroic
stature by defying fate and by being larger than life. A heroic
character could be good or evil, but he could never be ordinary. These concepts of heroism were in Melville's mind
when he created Captain Ahab, the larger-than-life whaling
captain who can be viewed as both the hero and the villain of
Moby-Dick.

Along with Shakespeare, Carlyle, and books of whaling
lore, Melville read a number of popular novels and dramas
while he was writing *Moby-Dick*. These books belonged to a
literary category called romance. In Melville's time, the term
"romance" did not mean a love story, as it does today. In the
nineteenth century, romances were stories that departed from
a realistic portrayal of life to deal with exaggerated or extreme
characters and events. Generally they involved an element of
mystery—sometimes even the supernatural. Romances often
featured heroes or villains who were intensely emotional, perhaps driven by the lust for power or revenge. Such tales frequently took place in exotic or wild settings. Some
romances—such as Ann Radcliffe's *The Mysteries of Udolpho*
(1794) and Sir Walter Scott's *Ivanhoe* (1819)—were among
the best-selling books of their time, and many writers tried to
produce books in this popular style. Melville's friend
Hawthorne experimented with romance in a story collection
called *Mosses from an Old Manse* (1846), in *The Scarlet Letter*,
and in a novel called *The House of the Seven Gables*, written
while Melville was writing *Moby-Dick* and published in 1851.
It is clear that Melville decided early in the writing of *Moby-
Dick* that his whaling book would be a romance—that is, a
tale of suspense, strangeness, and high emotion—instead of a
simple semi-autobiographical narrative like *Typee* or *Omoo*.

Moby-Dick took longer to write than any of Melville's
other books, partly because the book itself is long, but partly

because Melville's work was interrupted by many distractions. He started writing in the early spring of 1850. In May he told Richard Henry Dana, author of the sea story *Two Years Before the Mast*, that the book was half finished. In June he told his British publisher that the book would be done by the late autumn. But the summer of 1850 was filled with the move to Pittsfield and the visits and entertainments there. Despite these activities, Melville managed to get a great deal of writing done, and when Evert Duyckinck left Pittsfield to return to New York in August he reported to his brother that Melville's new book was "mostly done," calling it "a romantic, fanciful, literal and most enjoyable presentment of the Whale Fishery—something quite new."[2]

Then something happened that delayed the completion of *Moby-Dick* for another year. Although his failure to turn the book in on time angered his publishers and forced him to borrow money to pay his bills, Melville began to revise and expand the manuscript. Scholars who have studied Melville's life and work call this activity the "second growth" of *Moby-Dick*. It resulted in a book quite different from the one Melville had planned.

One reason Melville had to revise and expand the book was that his British publishers wanted it to be long enough to be issued in three volumes, the standard form of publication for important novels in Great Britain at the time. But that was not the only reason. Melville also wanted *Moby-Dick* to reflect all the new ideas and feelings he had around the time he moved to Pittsfield.

The year between August of 1850 and August of 1851 was a crucial time in Melville's life. It was as adventurous as any of the years he spent roaming the world's oceans, but now the adventure was happening inside Melville, in the inner world of ideas rather than the outer world of people and events.

Melville was stirred by the books he had been reading. He was excited by the idea that literature could probe into the deepest questions: What is reality? What is mankind's true nature? He longed to explore those questions himself.

Perhaps the single most important ingredient in Melville's intellectual ferment, though, was his friendship with Nathaniel Hawthorne. In late 1850 and early 1851 Melville exchanged several visits with Hawthorne and his family. Although Hawthorne seems to have been genuinely fond of Melville, the younger man's attachment to Hawthorne approached hero worship. In Hawthorne, Melville believed he saw proof that an American writer could achieve the level of genius demonstrated by Shakespeare and the other giants of European literature. And because he regarded his new friend as a creative genius, Melville may have felt ashamed of his two previous books, which he considered potboilers. His admiration for Hawthorne, combined with his newfound enthusiasm for serious literature, filled him with ambition. He wanted to show Hawthorne that he, too, could write a serious, imaginative book, a book that was deeply felt and not simply ground out for money.

Through the winter of 1850–51, while Melville revised his book, his determination kept the friendship with Hawthorne alive. On one occasion he traveled by sled to Lenox in the dead of winter to try to persuade Hawthorne to visit him. All through his life Melville was rather shy, and he was sometimes lonely for intellectual companionship and masculine camaraderie. For a time, it seemed that Hawthorne would fill that void.

The spring of 1851 brought new distractions: a garden to plant, troublesome bills to pay (Melville had to borrow money from the bank to do so), and the news that Elizabeth was expecting their second child in October. In a letter to

Nathaniel Hawthorne, author of The Scarlet Letter, *whose friendship stimulated Melville's intellect and imagination during the critical period when he was writing* Moby-Dick.

Hawthorne, Melville described his harassed state of mind as he struggled to finish the book:

In a week or so, I go to New York to bury myself in a third-story room, and work and slave on my "Whale" while it is driving through the press. That *is the only way I can finish it now,—I am so pulled hither and thither by circumstances. The calm, the coolness, the silent grass-growing mood in which a man* ought *always to compose,—that, I fear, can seldom be mine.*[3]

In the same letter, Melville complained that he felt torn between what he wanted to write and the sort of books that the public demanded. Perhaps he was remembering the failure of *Mardi*. "What I feel most moved to write, that is banned,—it will not pay," he wrote bitterly. "Yet, altogether write the *other* way I cannot. So the product is a final hash, and all my books are botches."[4]

Interestingly, this letter from the spring of 1851 shows that Melville had begun referring casually to his book as the "Whale" and not "the Whale fishery" as he had done earlier. In his original plan for the book, the dramatic conflict was to have been between a single-minded, tyrannical captain and a sensible, humane first mate. The whale—loosely based on the stories Melville had heard of Mocha Dick—was nothing more than a device to move the story along, something about which the captain and mate could argue. The final version of the book reflects traces of this first plan, for the white whale is not even mentioned until the end of the thirty-first chapter. But by the time the book was finally finished in July of 1851, the white whale of the title had become a character in its own right. In fact, it was the very center of the story.

Melville turned over the final pages of *Moby-Dick* to Harper and Brothers, dedicated the book to Hawthorne "in token of my admiration for his genius," and then sat back to see what the world would make of his epic.

9

"I HAVE WRITTEN A WICKED BOOK"

Many people did not know what to make of *Moby-Dick* when it was published in England and the United States in the fall of 1851. Richard Brodhead, a professor at Yale University who is one of the leading modern scholars of Melville, points out in his introduction to *New Essays on Moby-Dick* that Melville's novel confused readers because it did not fit neatly into a category they understood. Nineteenth-century readers expected a book to have a tidy label, called a genre. A book might belong to the genre of travel writing, or to the genre of moral allegory, or sea story, or tragic romance, or philosophical meditation, or prose epic—but certainly not to *all* of these categories, and more, at the same time.

In *Moby-Dick*, Melville created a one-of-a-kind book that mixed genres with abandon. Despite the failure of *Mardi*, which had proved unpopular largely because it appeared to blend several genres, Melville could not resist the creative urge to experiment with new things in *Moby-Dick*. He was inspired by the world of literary masterpieces in which he had

recently immersed himself. And he was filled with an aware-
ness that the act of writing a book was a form of exploration,
a journey of the mind that might lead him to an unknown
destination.

Studies of Moby-Dick have approached the book in a variety of ways—through its structure, style, characters, symbols,
and themes. But each of these approaches reveals a common
feature that is central to the book: the fact that nothing in
the world of Moby-Dick can be neatly labeled, that everything
has more than one possible meaning and interpretation. In
every aspect of his masterpiece, Melville tells us to shun easy
answers, formulaic responses, and obvious solutions. The universe, he says, is not that simple.

The plot of Moby-Dick seems straightforward enough on
the surface. A man named Ishmael, restless and in ill humor,
decides to enlist on a whaler. He explains his decision as a
way of escaping from his "hypos," or bad moods:

> Whenever I find myself growing grim about the mouth;
> whenever it is a damp, drizzly November in my soul;
> whenever I find myself involuntarily pausing before coffin
> warehouses, and bringing up the rear of every funeral I
> meet; and especially when my hypos get such an upper
> hand of me, that it requires a strong moral principle to pre-
> vent me from stepping into the street, and methodically
> knocking people's hats off—then, I account it high time to
> get to sea as soon as I can.[1]

This passage, which occurs on the first page of the book, uses
a device called foreshadowing. Melville employs foreshadowing throughout Moby-Dick. Foreshadowing is a way of setting
up the reader for what is to come. Images or events occur
more than once, and each time they acquire an additional

layer of meaning. In this case, Ishmael's reference to coffins foreshadows the last page of the book, when Ishmael clings to a coffin that keeps him afloat in the sea and saves his life. The reference to funerals is also a piece of foreshadowing, for there will be many deaths in the book.

In the New England whaling towns of New Bedford and Nantucket, Ishmael meets and befriends a South Seas islander named Queequeg, a harpooner. Together they sign on to the *Pequod*, which sails for the Pacific under Captain Ahab. The captain does not appear until the voyage is under way, and Ishmael then learns that he has an ivory leg. His leg was bitten off by Moby Dick, a huge white sperm whale, and now Ahab's sole ambition is to find and kill the white whale. After numerous incidents, including several whale kills and meetings with other ships, the *Pequod* sights Moby Dick. Ahab harpoons the whale, who smashes the hull of the *Pequod* with his mighty forehead. As the ship sinks and all the men drown, the harpoon line wraps around Ahab's neck, and the whale drags him to the depths. Only Ishmael, clinging to a floating coffin that had been built for his friend Queequeg, survives.

For such a seemingly simple story, *Moby-Dick* has a most complicated structure. It is impossible to know how much of the book's structural complexity is deliberate, and how much is the result of the way Melville changed his plans for the book as he went along, but *Moby-Dick* can be divided into three sections. The first 31 chapters introduce the characters and set the story in motion. The final chapters, from 106 to 135, cover the sighting of Moby Dick, the 3-day chase, and the fate of the *Pequod*. In between—the bulk of the novel—is a mass of chapters that move back and forth from the story of the *Pequod* and its crew to an account of the whaling industry and the natural history of whales. Melville gives us chapters on the whale in literature, mythology, and art; on every aspect of the whale's anatomy and way of life; on famous incidents involving ships and whales; and on the various steps in killing whales and producing oil. In fact, he very nearly gives us a textbook on whales and whaling as they were understood in the nineteenth century—except that no textbook would contain so much humor or such lavishly poetic language.

The "cetological center," as critics call the middle of *Moby-Dick* (cetology is the study of whales), has always been a point of dispute where the book's greatness is concerned. Some readers have found the book's structure peculiar and even annoying, as if a novel of seafaring adventure had been crossed with a science book to produce an unsatisfactory hybrid. Other readers have enjoyed the book's broad scope and its rambles through biology and geography. They feel that the cetological materials do not actually hurt the narrative. And still others admire the book's odd structure, feeling that Melville has enlarged our ideas of what a book can be. By mixing entire realms of scholarship, legend, action, and passion into *Moby-Dick*, Melville shows us that experience cannot be divided into watertight compartments. The cetological materials have another point, too, and it is an ironic one: Despite all the facts Melville musters, all the information he has gathered from the libraries of the world, he still cannot say exactly what the white whale is—and neither can the reader. Knowledge is entertaining, even useful, but it can go only so far. Then *imagination* must take over.

One aspect of structure that posed a few technical problems for Melville is point of view. A book's point of view is the viewpoint from which the story is told, usually either a character in the story or an impersonal narrator outside the story. *Moby-Dick* begins in the first person, giving Ishmael's point of view: "I did," "I said," and so on. Yet as the book expands, Ishmael's point of view is no longer enough. Some of the cetological chapters are told in the voice of a scholar or historian (and we have no reason to believe that Ishmael is either). Other chapters, more directly concerned with the action of the story, are about things that Ishmael could not possibly have witnessed: conversations between Ahab and his first mate alone in his cabin, for example, or glimpses into Ahab's thoughts. After such a chapter, Melville will suddenly drop back into Ishmael's point of view to describe an episode as the young sailor saw it. These shifts in point of view can be confusing to readers who expect the book to follow conventional rules.

Moby-Dick's style is as all-inclusive as its structure. Although the book does not contain actual poetry, it has a sample of just about every other kind of writing there is, including sermons, plays, encyclopedic information, long poetic speeches called soliloquies (typical of Shakespeare's tragedies), and suspense fiction. Although he was writing in the mid-nineteenth century, his approach to style was as modern as that of twentieth-century experimental novelists such as William Burroughs, who believe that style is flexible and infinitely individual. By switching styles and genres so freely, Melville points out that literature is no more fixed and definite than life itself.

Many of Melville's characters also prove the central principle of the book: that nothing has a single, fixed meaning. Queequeg, for example, is first presented as a fearsome savage, but Ishmael soon learns that Queequeg is a good, honorable, and affectionate man, more virtuous than many civilized folk.

Of all Melville's characters, Captain Ahab is the most ambiguous; he is the hardest to pin down to a single meaning. It is not even clear whether he is intended to be a hero or a villain. On one hand, he is insane, a victim of a mental disorder called monomania, which causes people to be obsessed with a single idea to the loss of all else. Ahab is obsessed with the dream of revenge against Moby Dick. His mental or spiritual imperfections are reflected in his physical appearance: in addition to his amputated leg, he bears a long, livid scar on his face.

Yet despite his madness and his flaws, Ahab has the same sort of appeal that is possessed by Satan in John Milton's famous religious poem *Paradise Lost*. He is a grand, heroic, passionate character who stirs our reluctant admiration because of his defiance and his insistence on forcing his will upon the universe. Ahab, like Satan, is determined to have his way even if it damns him. He refuses to recognize the existence of a higher law than his own will, and although this spiritual pride is destructive and dehumanizing, it also shows strength, determination, and imagination, all of which are attractive qualities. "I'd strike the sun if it insulted me," Ahab proudly tells Starbuck, the *Pequod*'s first mate, and the reader is both repelled and fascinated by his arrogance.

Other characters are somewhat less ambiguous. Starbuck is a calm, rational, practical man, brave without the recklessness of Ahab. He counsels moderation and prudence, only to be overridden by Ahab's monomania, as the voice of reason is often drowned out by madness or passion. Stubb, the second mate, is a jolly man of hearty appetites who likes to eat, drink, and laugh, but his fondness for sensual pleasures does not save him, any more than Starbuck's reasonableness saves him. Fedallah, Ahab's personal harpooner, is a mysterious and secretive Persian who may represent all that is worst in Ahab; he is the opposite of a guardian angel—he is a devil who whispers in Ahab's ear and directs him to damnation.

Moby-Dick is filled with symbols, entities that stand for— or symbolize—other entities. One of the main symbols is the

Pequod itself. As in some of Melville's earlier sea novels, especially *White-Jacket*, the ship is a symbol of the world, self-contained and moving through the sea as the world rolls through space. In this interpretation, the crew represents all of humanity. The ship's voyage, too, has symbolic meaning; literature is full of voyages that can be interpreted as symbols of lives, or journeys from birth to death with discoveries along the way.

Many ordinary objects in Melville's novel become symbolic. For example, Queequeg's coffin becomes a symbol first of death and then of life. Chapter 60, "The Line," appears on the surface to be a description of the rope that is attached to the harpoon. Below the surface, however, the rope has a symbolic meaning—it represents all the things that bind people, tie them down, and pull them through life. Melville brings this symbolism into the open at the end of the chapter:

> *But why say more? All men live enveloped in whale-lines. All are born with halters round their necks; but it is only when caught in the swift, sudden turn of death, that mortals realize the silent, subtle, everpresent perils of life. And if you be a philosopher, though seated in the whale-boat, you would not at heart feel one whit more of terror, than though seated before your evening fire with a poker, and not a harpoon, by your side.* [2]

In addition to its symbolism, this passage is a good example of foreshadowing. It hints at the way Ahab will die, seized around the neck by the whale-line.

The sea is an important symbol throughout the book, and one that reinforces the principle of multiple meanings. At the beginning of the novel, Ishmael turns to the sea as a source of rebirth and renewal, but later he sees that it is also a dangerous place that can be a realm of death. He describes it as beautiful, shaded with "the loveliest tints of azure," but it is also a wild place filled with "universal cannibalism," where all creatures "prey upon each other, carrying on eternal war since the world began." The ambiguous nature of the sea is shown in Chapter 93, "The Castaway," in which Pip, the young African-American cabin boy, falls out of a whaleboat and is abandoned in the middle of the ocean during the whale chase. He is later picked up, but the experience has left him insane, babbling and laughing like a child. Pip symbolizes the power of the sea both to terrify and destroy men and also to return them to a state of childlike innocence.

The most important—and most ambiguous—symbol in *Moby-Dick* is Moby Dick himself. Generations of readers and critics have asked: What does the great white whale represent? Throughout the novel, characters debate this issue in an echo of the sailors' debates about the sinking of the *Essex* that Melville heard on the *Acushnet* years earlier. Is Moby Dick a cruel, savage beast who attacked Ahab deliberately? Or is he, as Starbuck believes, nothing more than an animal, innocent of good or evil intentions? To Ahab, the whale is more than just an object of hatred. It is a symbol of everything that is out of the individual's control and beyond his knowledge. Ahab burns to kill Moby Dick partly for revenge, but also because he cannot bear the thought that there are forces greater than he is.

Yet the white whale can be interpreted in many ways. In traditional Christian symbolism, white is the color of purity and goodness, and some critics have seen Moby Dick as an emblem of religious faith, or even as Jesus. Others have interpreted the whale as death, the unavoidable fate of all who sail the sea of life. To others, Moby Dick represents the physical world, which can destroy man but does so mindlessly, not by evil intent. In recent years, scholars have begun to study *Moby-Dick* within its historical context, and they see the whale as Melville's symbol of nature, relentlessly pursued by industrial technology. This interpretation reflects a modern disenchantment with the changes brought by the Industrial Revolution; it echoes environmentalists' fears that we have become alienated from the natural world and are destroying it through our own actions.

Melville gives one clue to the meaning of the whale in Chapter 74, which discusses the anatomy of the sperm whale's head. He tells us that because the whale's eyes are set on opposite sides of its head, it sees two separate images at one time, unlike human beings, who look straight ahead. Many critics see this as Melville's statement that the book is about the need to see that everything has multiple meanings. The whale perceives the world in terms of dualities, or double images, while people see only one thing at a time. Ahab, driven by monomania, has the narrowest vision of all, and it proves to be his undoing. Melville seems to be saying that, unlike man, the whale knows that reality is not a single picture but is made up of many layers of meaning.

Melville's lengthiest account of the meaning of the whale occurs in Chapter 42, called "The Whiteness of the Whale." Here the narrator meditates on the significance of the color white. He admits that in many cultures whiteness stands for joy, cleanliness, and goodness, but then he explains that whiteness can also be seen as an empty, frightening blankness, a void in which nothing has form or meaning, a "monumental white shroud." This interpretation of whiteness strikes at one of the central themes of the book, the search for meaning. In seeking to pierce Moby Dick with his harpoon, Ahab is trying to pierce through the blank white veil of matter that hides the true meaning of the universe. He wants to pass beyond the normal limits of human knowledge and experience, to solve the great mystery of life's purpose. But is there anything beyond the veil? "Sometimes I think there's naught beyond," Ahab says in a moment of dark doubt. This speculation echoes a comment Melville made in a letter: "And perhaps, after all, there is *no* secret."[3]

"There is *no* secret"—that may be the secret of *Moby-Dick*. Melville had become skeptical about the standard answers offered by religion, science, and social values to questions about life's meaning. Had he lived in the twentieth century, Melville might have been called an existentialist, one who believes that the universe is unfathomable and that individuals must take responsibility for their own actions rather than being guided by some formal system of rights and wrongs. In *Moby-Dick*, Melville explored the possibility that there *is* no meaning, no eternal truth beyond the visible, material world. Christians would consider such views blasphemous, as Melville well knew. He had been baptized and brought up in the Dutch Reformed Church, like all Maria Melville's children, but he had become skeptical of systems of belief—including organized religions—that claimed to offer the absolute truth about the meaning of life. He knew, however, that such skepticism would be ill received by conventional readers such as Evert Duyckinck. Melville confessed privately to Hawthorne, "I have written a wicked book." Yet it is important to note that Melville does not say that there is no God. He merely wonders whether God does exist and how much we can really know of God's ways. It is Ahab, who denies the existence of God or of any being who is wiser or more powerful than himself, who is destroyed. Ishmael, who humbly casts himself on the mercy of the sea and admits his weakness, survives to tell the tale.

One other theme in *Moby-Dick* deserves attention: the

contrast between isolation and community. Next to his monomania, Ahab's chief characteristic is his isolation from other people. Not until late in the novel do we learn that he has a wife and child ashore whom he has abandoned to search for the white whale. He keeps himself apart from the rest of the crew and considers himself superior to everyone else: "Kneel, dog," he orders Stubb, the second mate, on one occasion. This self-imposed exile from the human race is contrasted with the friendship between Ishmael and Queequeg and with other scenes of fellowship among the crewmen of the *Pequod.*

Ahab's most violent rejection of the ties of shared humanity occurs when the *Pequod* is stopped by another ship, the *Rachel,* and asked to help search for one of the *Rachel's* missing whaleboats that contains the captain's young son. "Do as you would have me do to you in the like case," pleads Captain Gardiner of the *Rachel.* "For *you* too have a boy, Captain Ahab." But Ahab has learned that the *Rachel* had encountered Moby Dick, and he refuses to help in the search. His only thought is to pursue the whale at once. "Captain Gardiner, I will not do it," he replies coldly. "Even now I lose time."

His refusal to show compassion and to share the universal human burden of caring for another person dooms Ahab. If he had joined the *Rachel* in the search for the lost youth, he would perhaps not have caught up with Moby Dick and with his own grim destiny. But although one son is lost, another is found. Queequeg and all Ishmael's other shipmates perish in the wreck, and Ishmael is left alone in the middle of the sea, "another orphan," as he calls himself. Ironically, it is the *Rachel* that finally rescues him and carries him back to the world of men. Ishmael came close to perishing alone in the empty sea, but he was saved in time by a compassionate captain. The links of care and kindness between human beings are frail, Melville seems to be saying, but ultimately they are the only thing we can rely upon in this life, and they are our only sure salvation.

10

MELVILLE'S CRISIS

In the months after Melville finished writing *Moby-Dick*, his life was full of events, some happy, some sad. His second child was born in October of 1851; he and Elizabeth named the boy Stanwix. They were to have two more children, both girls. Elizabeth was born in 1853, and Frances in 1856. But Stanwix's birth was hard on Melville's wife. In addition, she was growing bored with life at Arrowhead. Claiming poor health, she went to her parents' home in Boston for a long visit during the winter.

Melville suffered a personal loss in November of 1851, when the Hawthornes, tired of life in the Berkshires and pressed with financial problems, moved away to Concord, outside of Boston. Two years later, when Hawthorne was appointed to a diplomatic job in Liverpool, they moved to England. After Nathaniel Hawthorne left Lenox, Melville saw him only a few times. The friendship that had started out so warmly faded into a more distant feeling of good will. Hawthorne liked and admired Melville, but the friendship simply did not thrive once Melville was no longer able to cul-

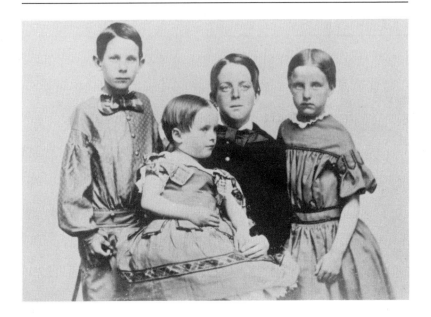

The children of Herman and Elizabeth Melville: (left to right) Stanwix, Frances, Malcolm, and Elizabeth.

tivate it with frequent visits. Melville's letters and other writings show that he was deeply depressed by the loss of the close bond he had felt with Hawthorne.

Another source of anxiety in late 1851 was the appearance in print of *Moby-Dick*. Melville hoped that both the literary critics and the reading public would give the book a favorable—and profitable—reception. Just as the book came out, Evert Duyckinck sent Melville a newspaper article about the *Ann Alexander*, a New Bedford whaler that was rammed and sunk by a sperm whale, and Melville excitedly wondered whether the incident would boost the sales of his book. "I wonder," he wrote with tongue in cheek, "if my evil art has raised this monster."[1]

All too soon he discovered that nothing could boost sales

of *Moby-Dick*. The first few reviews were good; one critic wrote approvingly that the book was "not a mere tale of adventures, but a whole philosophy of life." Yet for every positive review there were two negative ones. Some reviewers, baffled or offended by the book, called Melville insane or immoral. One of the most hurtful reviews came from Duyckinck, who took Melville to task for criticizing or mocking religion and social standards. This stuffy, priggish review strained the friendship between Melville and Duyckinck; the two had little contact for several years afterward. But Melville was thrilled to receive praise from Hawthorne and his wife, both of whom admired *Moby-Dick* very much.

Sadly, the reading public did not share the Hawthornes' enthusiasm. The book sold fewer than two thousand copies. In comparison, Harriet Beecher Stowe's novel *Uncle Tom's Cabin*, published the following year, sold hundreds of thousands of copies and remained a best-seller for the rest of the nineteenth century, while *Moby-Dick* was first ignored and then forgotten. A stricken Melville faced the fact that once again, and despite his best effort, success had eluded him.

Money problems began to press urgently upon Melville. He had a wife and two children to support, and he was also responsible for much of the day-to-day support of his mother and sisters. His only sources of income were farming and writing, and farming did not produce much cash, so he returned to his writing desk. He was still convinced he could produce a book that would have popular appeal.

The book he produced was called *Pierre*. It was intended to be a romance—a novel of mystery and sentimental emotion—modeled to some extent on Hawthorne's *The Scarlet Letter* and *The House of the Seven Gables*. Melville also intended that *Pierre* should appeal to women, as he believed that few women, or none, had responded to the exclusively masculine world of *Moby-Dick*. (Some critics have suggested that there are no women in *Moby-Dick* because Melville was rather oppressed by his houseful of women and used his whaling novel as an escape from the feminine atmosphere.)

Pierre is the story of two young lovers, Pierre and Lucy, whose engagement is broken when a dark, mysterious young woman named Isabel appears and claims to be Pierre's illegitimate half sister. Isabel is an outcast without a place in the world, and Pierre nobly decides to marry her in order to give her a respectable position. He is the only one who knows that she is really his sister, and the two agree to live together as brother and sister rather than as husband and wife. Melville might have been able to make a sentimental romance out of this story, but he could not resist the urge to add many digressions about morality, society, and love. Melville thought that *Pierre* was "very much more calculated for popularity" than any of his books since *Omoo*, and he confidently predicted great commercial success for it.

While waiting for his publishers to make him an offer for *Pierre*, Melville had a short break from routine in the summer of 1852. His father-in-law, Judge Shaw, took him on a tour of New Bedford and Nantucket. Melville thoroughly enjoyed the trip and heard a number of tales about sailors and the sea that he thought he might someday use in a book. One story particularly interested Melville: the tale of a Quaker woman who had been deserted by her husband and had patiently borne her desertion, only to see her husband return years later with another wife. Melville wrote to Hawthorne, suggesting that Hawthorne might want to use this story as the basis for a novel, but Hawthorne politely returned the idea to Melville—who never did make use of it. While in Nantucket, Melville also met and talked with Captain Pollard, the man who had been in command of the *Essex* when that ship was sunk by the sperm whale. The author of *Moby-Dick* naturally had much to discuss with this maritime veteran, whom he had mentioned by name in the novel.

Upon returning to Arrowhead, Melville learned that Harpers had agreed to publish *Pierre*, but Melville received only $500 for it; at the time he owed the publishers $150 for books he had bought from them. Neither Harpers nor Melville's British publisher seemed to think much of the book's chances, and as it turned out, they were right. When it appeared later in 1852, the book sold only 238 copies in 8 months—a dismal record. It was almost universally condemned by reviewers, who were put off by the book's high-flown philosophy and scandalized by the hints of an incestuous attraction between Pierre and Isabel. Evert Duyckinck, who had grown increasingly critical of Melville, went so far as to suggest that Melville had gone insane.

Now Melville entered a period of considerable stress and unhappiness. He had written seven books in eight years, with a period of especially hard, sustained work from 1849 through 1852, when five of his novels appeared. He was deeply downcast that his three most ambitious books—*Mardi*, *Moby-Dick* and *Pierre*—had failed to win the esteem he had expected for them. Although he was not reduced to real poverty and at times even managed to have a little money in the bank, he was constantly worried about finances. Frequently he had to rely on loans and gifts of money from his father-in-law and other relatives to support himself and his family.

Melville's domestic life, too, was a source of distress. His marriage had become tense and rather unhappy, for Elizabeth did not approve of her husband's dedication to literature. She was inclined to mother Melville and to boss him—treatment he already received in abundance from his mother—and she felt that such sustained writing was bad for him. And if he *had* to write, she added, why not write another *Typee*, or some other easy, uncontroversial, profitable book? Around this time Elizabeth and Maria Melville, together with some of Melville's other relatives, began busying themselves trying to get Melville a job in the diplomatic service. Hawthorne had been made the United States consul, or diplomatic representative, in Liverpool. Could a similar job be found for Melville? If Melville obtained such a post, Maria Melville firmly announced, she would keep her grandchildren at home with her while Melville and Elizabeth moved abroad. This prospect upset Melville, who was always lonely for his children whenever he was away from them, but in the end the idea came to nothing. Despite all Maria Melville's meddlesome attempts to organize her son's life, no consular post was offered to Melville.

On top of his other troubles, Melville began to suffer from a variety of health problems. His eyesight was getting worse, and he had developed rheumatism, neuralgia (severe headaches), and sciatica (pain in the back and hips). Writing became difficult and even, at times, physically painful. Yet Melville felt compelled to keep writing.

Starting in 1853, he took up a new form of literary activity, perhaps hoping to avoid the kind of books that had turned readers and critics against him. Instead of novels, he began to produce stories and essays for two magazines, *Harper's* and *Putnam's Monthly*. Some of these stories contain clues about how Melville felt at this point in his life about himself, his career, and his family. They are about characters who achieve contentment only when they give up worldly ambition. The hero of "The Fiddler" is a violin-player who becomes famous as a child prodigy, then falls into neglect and obscurity in his adulthood. However, he is happier once he is no longer striving for fame. "The Happy Failure" is about an inventor who is obsessed with making a successful invention. He devotes all his energy and passion to this quest, and only when it fails does he gain peace of mind. These stories may be seen as Melville's rejection of ambition, or possibly as his attempt to convince himself that he was better off without fame.

Other stories of this period concern characters who are perverse, who defy common sense and the logic of ordinary behavior. They stubbornly and silently go their own ways, doing what they feel compelled to do, in spite of all attempts to make them change their courses. The best-known of these is "Bartleby the Scrivener" (a scrivener is a copyist—the job Melville's friend Fly had gotten in New York after their western trip, and the one Melville had failed to get because of his poor handwriting). Bartleby is one of the story's two main characters; the other is the lawyer who employs him. Calm and self-contained, Bartleby suffers from an emotional disorder that causes him to withdraw from the world in stages. At first he startles the lawyer by occasionally saying "I would prefer not to" when he is told to perform some task. These refusals, always bland and polite, increase in frequency, and the lawyer notices that Bartleby's behavior is strange in other ways as well. The scrivener seems to have no friends or family and to live in the office at night. The lawyer tries to help and encourage Bartleby but receives no response. Finally, driven to distraction by Bartleby's impenetrable stubbornness, the lawyer moves to another office. Bartleby remains fixedly in the old office until he is arrested and sent to prison, where he dies—apparently by choice. The story defies easy interpretation. Is Bartleby insane? Or is he more sane than those around him because he realizes that the common fate of all mankind is isolation and death?

"I and My Chimney" also tackles the theme of stubborn

immovability, but in a cheerful way. It is a humorous sketch, or essay, rather than a fictional story. Melville describes the huge fireplace and chimney at Arrowhead, the most notable feature of the house, and his wife's vigorous efforts to tear down the chimney and otherwise remodel the house. Although the sketch is lighthearted and genial in tone, there seems to be a touch of bitter irony in Melville's portrayal of himself as a meek, henpecked man in a house full of over-bearing women. This was a condition that mirrored his real life, at least to some extent. In the sketch, however, Melville steadfastly defends the old chimney, saying that although it may not be new or efficient, it gets the job done. And he manages to keep the wife from tearing it down. Some critics believe that the chimney represents Melville's writing career. The stubborn and perverse characters in these magazine pieces may reflect Melville's own quiet determination to per-sist as a writer, and to do so on his own terms.

The most important of the works that Melville produced during this period of magazine writing was *Benito Cereno*, which is a novella or short novel rather than a true short story. It is based on a true incident about which Melville read in a book called *Narrative of Voyages and Travels*, published in 1817 by a sea captain named Amasa Delano. The captain recalled meeting a Spanish ship in the waters off Chile in 1809. The ship was a slave ship. It had been loaded with a cargo of African slaves, who had seized control of the vessel in a violent rebellion. Delano had recaptured the ship and turned the rebellious slaves over to the Spanish authorities in Chile, where their leaders were executed.

Although he used the real name Amasa Delano for his story's narrator, Melville fictionalized the original incident to some extent, heightening its dramatic tension and adding horrific symbolism. *Benito Cereno* is noteworthy for Melville's rich, elaborate use of language, by which he creates a mood of terror and suspense similar to that found in the gothic horror stories of Edgar Allan Poe, another great nineteenth-century American writer. Benito Cereno, the title character, is the captain of the Spanish ship *San Dominick*. He is a doomed and helpless figure who witnessed the mutilation and death of his friend, the slave trader who owned the ship's human cargo and then fell under the control of his own servant.

One of the tale's themes is the contrast between appearance and reality, especially as seen through the eyes of Delano, who misunderstands and misinterprets everything he sees aboard the ship until he, too, is in mortal danger. Another theme is the difficulty of identifying good and evil. The slaves who plot and carry out the revolt demonstrate great cruelty, cunning, and malice. But slave trading is also shown in all its evil inhumanity. The reader is left unsure of who is a villain and who a hero, who is a master and who a slave. As in *Moby-Dick*, Melville recognized the ambiguity of moral situations. The only thing that seems clear is that each inhumane act degrades everyone it touches, both the victim of the act and the person who commits it.

Benito Cereno is timeless in its meaning, but it can also be read as a document of its time—specifically of the 1850s, years when the debate over slavery was rising to fever pitch. The conflict between slaveholders and abolitionists was threatening to tear the United States apart and was one of the causes of the Civil War that was soon to engulf the nation. When Melville wrote *Benito Cereno*, many countries had already outlawed slavery, and by emphasizing Delano's inability to understand the tragedy that had occurred on the slave ship, Melville may be making a point about America's naive backwardness where the issue of slavery was concerned.

In 1855, Melville published *Israel Potter*, the story he had planned a few years earlier about the veteran of the American Revolution who spent decades as an exile in England. The book was serialized in Putnam's magazine—published chapter by chapter over a series of issues—and then released as a book. It did not arouse much excitement among readers in either form. But although it is not regarded as one of Melville's major works, *Israel Potter* is a competently written historical adventure novel. It is interesting today for its portraits of real-life characters such as Benjamin Franklin and John Paul Jones.

The following year, 1856, brought the publication of a collection of Melville's short works under the title *The Piazza Tales* (a piazza is a terrace or patio, and Melville had built one on the north side of Arrowhead, where he could sit and think and write). By the time the story collection appeared, Melville was already at work on a new novel, forging steadily ahead despite bouts of depression and ill health. As he had done so often before, he turned to an adventure in his past for subject matter. This time he recalled his youthful journey down a stretch of the Mississippi River. The setting for the novel was a steamer trip down the Mississippi. Melville called the book *The Confidence-Man*. He did not know it, but it would be the last novel published during his lifetime.

A confidence man, or con man, is a trickster who takes advantage of others by persuading them to trust him and then defrauding them. The central character of *The Confidence-Man* is just such a deceiver, who appears in a variety of different disguises. The book is a series of vignettes, or separate scenes, and may have been planned as a collection of sketches or stories rather than as a novel. Each vignette takes the steamboat to a new stretch of river and provides the confidence man with new victims to fleece. The book begins as playful, humorous satire but takes on a grim, cynical tone as

Melville shows one instance after another of human foolishness. As he did in *Benito Cereno*, Melville explored the idea that nothing is what it seems to be. People who seem wise turn out to be gullible, and those who seem trustworthy turn out to be cheats.

By the time Melville finished writing *The Confidence-Man*, he was in poor physical and psychological health. Some biographers have said that he suffered a nervous breakdown in the spring and summer of 1856. His true state of mental and physical health is not known for sure, but at the very least he was worn out from overwork, disappointment, and stress. His wife was worried about him. Furthermore, she had no taste for another long winter in the Berkshires, shut up in a snowbound house with four children. But she knew that Melville's pride and his quiet stubbornness would prevent him from spending the season with any of his relatives or hers. Therefore she persuaded her father that Melville needed a trip abroad to restore his health. Judge Shaw agreed to pay for a trip, and Elizabeth arranged to spend the winter in Boston with her children while Melville toured Europe and the Holy Land (as the modern state of Israel was often called during the nineteenth century).

Melville agreed to these arrangements without hesitation. Perhaps he did not know that his wife and mother were determined to wean him from writing and hoped to line up a job for him while he was away from home. Perhaps he did not care, and simply yearned for a change of scene and routine.

He left Pittsfield in September of 1856, soon after his thirty-seventh birthday. He was bound once again for England and points beyond, and he carried with him a copy of the manuscript of *The Confidence-Man*, hoping to sell it to a British publisher. On the way, Melville stopped in New York to call on Evert Duyckinck. The visit was the first step in rebuilding their friendship, and it was a sign that Melville hoped to heal some of the stress and unhappiness that had overshadowed his life in the previous few years. He was seeking inner peace, and one way to achieve it was to make peace with the people in his life.

Several days later, Melville's ship, the *Glasgow*, pulled away from New York harbor. The *Glasgow* was a steamship. Even if Melville had wanted to spring into the rigging with his former youthful energy, he could not have done so, for there was no rigging. The weary Melville probably did not miss these aerial acrobatics. Yet despite the crushing disappointments of recent years, Melville retained some enthusiasm. At last he would see Turkey, and Jerusalem, and the pyramids—sights he had been unable to afford on his 1849 trip to Europe. He leaned on the ship's rail and looked ahead with tired but hopeful eyes.

11

THE QUIET YEARS

Melville's trip began with a tour of Scotland, the home of his father's ancestors. Then he journeyed south to Liverpool for a reunion with Hawthorne, whom he had not seen in some time. The two men had drifted apart. In fact, Melville did not even know that Hawthorne had moved to a new house a year and a half earlier, and it took him some time to track down Hawthorne's new address. When the two men finally met, however, their friendship rekindled. They walked on the beach and talked about God, and knowledge, and the universe, and other lofty subjects, and Melville was left with the feeling that they had recaptured, however briefly, some of their former comradeship.

Hawthorne described Melville at that time as "looking much as he used to do (a little paler, and perhaps a little sadder), in a rough outside coat, and with his characteristic gravity and reserve of manner."[1] With penetrating insight, he saw that the root of much of Melville's unhappiness was his loss of faith. Melville's years of observation, study, and reflection had made him question religious beliefs and social standards that many people accepted without thought. Yet although Melville's mind told him to reject certain beliefs, his heart was troubled. Said Hawthorne:

> *He can neither believe; nor be comfortable in his unbelief; and he is too honest and courageous not to try to do one or the other. If he were a religious man, he would be one of the most truly religious and reverential; he has a very high and noble nature, and better worth immortality than most of us.*[2]

Leaving Liverpool and Hawthorne, Melville sailed to Constantinople (now Istanbul). Along the way he passed through the Mediterranean Sea and was struck by the beauty of Spain and especially of Greece. Constantinople, an ancient metropolis where Europe and Asia met and mingled in teeming streets and bazaars, seemed to him crowded and rather frightening, but he enjoyed Egypt, his next stop. The most thrilling experience of the whole trip was seeing the pyramids at Giza, outside Cairo. Their timeless mystery filled Melville with awe. He climbed to the top of one—pausing several times to catch his breath—and surveyed the view.

He next toured the biblical cities of Jericho and Jerusalem, where he was as much interested in the American and European tourists he met as in the dusty antiquities that surrounded him. He found the landscape of the Holy Land bleak and barren, but he studied the different ways in which devoutly religious people and doubters reacted to such sights as the places where Jesus was said to have been born and died. He decided that these places had a powerful effect on everyone, even on unbelievers, because they were loaded with centuries of tradition and legend. Melville had been

When he fulfilled his old dream of visiting Egypt, Melville climbed one of the pyramids. Like other Americans, citizens of a young nation, he was impressed by their great antiquity.

hoping that the trip would restore the simple, unquestioning religious faith of his childhood, but it did not. He was, as he wrote in his journal, "afflicted with the great curse of modern travel—skepticism."

He moved on to Greece, where he spent several days among the ruins of the ancient Greek civilization, and then to Italy. His spirits rose among the imperial ruins and art treasures of Rome and other cities, but his health began to trouble him, and he suffered from eyestrain and rheumatism. As soon as he felt well enough to travel again, he journeyed north by train, horseback, and carriage through Switzerland, Germany, and the Netherlands, eventually reaching England in April of 1857. After pilgrimages to such popular attractions as Shakespeare's birthplace, he paid a farewell visit to Hawthorne and set sail from Liverpool for New York and home.

Melville hoped that the sights he had seen and the thoughts he had pondered during the trip would produce another novel. His relatives hoped that the trip had put him in a good mood so that he would seek a job and give up writing. Neither of these hopes came true at once.

While Melville was away, his wife and mother had tried to get him a position in the New York customs house, the agency that collected customs, or import taxes, on cargoes brought into New York City. Politicians rewarded their friends and supporters with such jobs, but Melville simply did not have enough influence to get one.

The Confidence-Man was published in both England and America in 1857. Some English critics liked it; the American critics, however, found it bitter and distasteful. Melville's brother-in-law privately dismissed the book as "that horribly nonsensical class of books he is given to writing—where there are pages of crude theory and speculation to every line of narrative—and interspersed with strained and ineffectual attempts to be humorous."[3] Critics today have a higher appreciation of *The Confidence-Man*. Although it is not as smoothly written or profound as Melville's best works, it is worth reading as a satire on human folly. It stands in the tradition of nineteenth-century works of biting irony about human nature that includes Mark Twain's *The Mysterious Stranger*.

Melville's career as a writer had started with surprising success. Then—at least in terms of popularity and income—it had gone steadily downhill. He had endured a series of disappointments over *Mardi*, *Moby-Dick*, and *Pierre*. At the same time, writing had become physically and emotionally painful for him. Now the failure of *The Confidence-Man* left him with little desire to start a new novel. When his American publishers went out of business a few months later he gave up all thoughts of continuing to earn his living with his pen.

He had to do *something*, however, so he decided to take up lecturing. In the nineteenth century, lectures by authors, travelers, and other figures of public interest were a major form of entertainment. Successful lecturers were highly regarded. Melville was sufficiently well known to draw at least a modest crowd—although most people came to see the South Seas adventurer rather than the author of philosophical novels.

Melville's lecturing career started well. He sought advice from a successful lecturer and booked himself on a tour through New England and the Midwest. His topic was "The Statues of Rome"—a subject in which Melville had developed great interest, but one that perplexed listeners who had expected to hear about the Pacific. During his second season of lecturing he spoke on "The South Seas" and was well received. But Melville did not enjoy either giving lectures or being away from his children while on tour. His third season, during which he lectured on "Traveling," was a failure. His lack of enthusiasm was so obvious that one newspaper declared indignantly: "No man has a right to set himself up as a lecturer at $50 per night, who cannot for one minute take his eyes from his manuscript." Melville gave only three speeches that year and then retired from lecturing.

Melville's brother Thomas, who had gone to sea as a boy after hearing about Herman's adventures, was now the captain of the *Meteor*, a tall-masted clipper ship bound from New York around Cape Horn to San Francisco. The clipper ships, developed by American shipbuilders in the 1850s for the China trade, were the fastest and perhaps the finest ships that had ever been built. Thomas invited Melville to make the voyage as his guest, and Melville, perhaps longing to see the

Pacific again, accepted. He sailed with Thomas from May to November of 1860 and then returned to New York from San Francisco, to be greeted by a familiar chorus.

Once again his wife and relatives urged him to seek a job through political appointment. They felt that he should have a consular job like the one Hawthorne had obtained in Liverpool. At long last, Melville stopped resisting their plans, for after more than a decade of exhausting literary labors he had run dry. He was on the verge of asking for the job of consul in Glasgow, Scotland, when two things happened that changed his course of action. First, his father-in-law died, leaving Elizabeth Melville a modest legacy that would allow the family to live in comfort and financial security. They used some of the money to rent a house in New York City so that Elizabeth would not have to spend the winter of 1860–61 in isolation at Arrowhead.

The second event of this period changed not just Melville's plans but the history of the United States: North and South went to war in the spring of 1861. Stirred by patriotic feelings, Melville tried to enlist in the Union navy but was turned down because of his poor health.

The Melvilles spent most of the war years (1861–65) in New York. Melville was ready to move back into the city. He tried several times to sell Arrowhead—once to the county for use as a lunatic asylum—but could not find a buyer. In November 1862 he was thrown from a horse-drawn wagon and suffered a broken shoulder and other injuries; for months afterward he was quiet and moody. Finally, in 1863 he traded Arrowhead to his brother Allan for Allan's house on East Twenty-sixth Street in New York.

The move to New York improved Melville's spirits and restored his energy. Like all Americans, he took a keen interest in the progress of the war. He and Allan obtained a government permit to visit the battlefields and traveled to the scene of the fighting south of Washington, D.C. Legend says that Melville even went along on a brief scouting trip into Confederate territory, but there is no way to know whether this story is fact or fiction. We do know that Melville thought much about the war and the tragic sights he had seen, for during the war he began writing again. This time he produced neither novels nor short stories but poems, many dealing with patriotic or military subjects. "The March to the Sea," "Gettysburg," and other poems were published in magazines, and although Melville received little money for them, literary critics as well as his own friends and relatives seemed to approve.

Such approval was particularly welcome by the mid-1860s, when Melville often felt hurt by public neglect. He was sad when he thought of the bright literary future he had planned for himself only to see his early fame fade, and he could not help occasional pangs of jealousy when he saw the high regard in which other authors were held. In 1866 he collected his poems and published them as a book called *Battle-Pieces and Aspects of the War*. Published in 1866, when the wounds of the war were still raw, Melville's book of poetry showed his support of and pride in the Union, but it also showed sympathy for the ravaged South. Unfortunately, the book was a commercial failure. Fewer than five hundred copies were sold in eight years. Melville had paid for the publication of the book, hoping that it would prove profitable, but he lost four hundred dollars on the transaction.

By the end of the war, Melville was ready to settle down into the sort of steady job that his wife and mother had always wanted for him. He did not desperately need a salary, but everyone agreed that regular hours and structured employment would be good for his health and might keep him from brooding about his writing. The war, along with a series of scandals, had dispersed the staff of the New York customs house, and jobs were available. Melville applied for one, was accepted, and began his career as a deputy inspector of customs—in reality a glorified clerk's position—in December of 1866. He was paid four dollars a day, an amount about equal to what Elizabeth received from her inheritance. The family of six could live comfortably, if not opulently, on this income, and for the first time Melville felt a measure of financial security.

He was to spend nearly twenty years at the customs house. For the most part, they were quiet, uneventful years. But the Melvilles did experience several family tragedies during this time. The first occurred in 1867, when Melville's older son, Malcolm, was living in his parents' home in New York. A high-spirited, rebellious young man, Malcolm had joined a Union militia band during the war and had taken up the habit of carrying a loaded pistol and sleeping with it under his pillow. One September day in 1867 he was found shot to death by his own hand. It was never clear whether Malcolm's death was an accident or suicide, but its effect on Melville and Elizabeth was devastating. Melville agonized over his relationship with his son, fearing that he had been too strict a father, and Elizabeth blamed herself for spoiling the boy.

Stanwix, or Stanny, their second son, also brought grief and worry into their lives. Like Melville, he was unable to settle on a career, but he was more restless and unstable than his father. He worked briefly as a legal clerk, a sailor, a farmer, and a dentist before going to California in the 1870s to try sheepherding and then prospecting. Stanwix had little contact with his parents in the years before his death in a San Francisco hospital in 1886. By then Melville had also lost his brother Allan, his mother, his favorite sister Augusta, and his uncle Peter Gansevoort, who had been a friend since Herman's boyhood.

It was to Peter Gansevoort's generosity, in fact, that Melville owed the publication of his last significant work, a book-length poem called *Clarel: A Poem and Pilgrimage in the Holy Land*. He had begun writing in 1870, slowly piecing together 18,000 lines about his impressions from the trip of 1856–57. The poem's hero is a young man named Clarel who travels through the Holy Land, searching for something to believe in. He seeks the meaning of life in religion, science, love, and material possessions, but the only result of his spiritual quest is the realization that the battle of faith against despair takes place constantly in all human souls. No belief can be absolutely certain. The poem's final verses express Melville's ultimate uncertainty about whether or not there is a God who gives meaning to the universe:

> Yea, ape and angel, strife and old debate—
> The harps of heaven and the dreary gongs of hell;
> Science the feud can only aggravate—
> No umpire she betwixt the chimes and knell:
> The running battle of the star and clod
> Shall run for ever—if there be no God.[4]

Melville was fairly certain that no publisher would be interested in issuing the poem, so Peter Gansevoort, who had always respected his nephew's genius, gave Melville twelve hundred dollars to pay for its publication. Gansevoort died on the very day the arrangements for publication were completed. *Clarel*'s only readers today are scholars of Melville's life and works. It belongs to a type of literature that has gone out of fashion: the philosophical verse epic. A few such poems, including Alfred Tennyson's *In Memoriam*, were widely read in the nineteenth century, but *Clarel* held little appeal for critics and readers when it appeared in 1875.

The decade after the publication of *Clarel* passed quietly. Melville went to work at the customs house in the morning and came home at night. He tended his rose garden and proudly displayed the blooms to friends and neighbors. He also vacationed with his wife and daughters in the Berkshires or the White Mountains of New Hampshire. He passed many genial evenings with his old friend Evert Duyckinck, with whom he was reconciled, until Duyckinck's death in 1877. In 1879 Elizabeth inherited money from her stepmother; she gave her husband an allowance of twenty-five dollars a month especially to buy books. Melville, too, came into a modest inheritance from one of his sisters. Financially secure at last, he left the customs house in 1885 and settled into dignified retirement.

Herman Melville was now sixty-six years old, tired and rather feeble, and almost forgotten. When he settled into his quiet study to "put his papers in order," no one suspected that in the twilight of his life, with his writing career long behind him, Melville would write another masterpiece.

12

NEGLECT AND REDISCOVERY

Melville's granddaughter Eleanor, in a book about her grandfather that was published in 1953, described him in his years of retirement. He spent a lot of time, she said, sitting on a narrow porch that ran across the back of his New York home, gazing thoughtfully at his garden and smoking his pipe.[1] He did little traveling after leaving the customs house: a few vacations to the seashore or the mountains with Elizabeth, and one last sea voyage to Bermuda and Florida in 1888. The seas were rough, and Melville—who had once ridden out storms in the rigging of sailing ships—had to crawl about the deck on his hands and knees. He reflected ruefully and with gentle humor on the changes brought about by age and the passage of time.

Melville's public career as an author was long over, but he had never stopped writing. Once he had rid himself of the driving pressure to succeed for financial reasons, he continued to write for his own self-expression. Now that he had retired, he spent many hours at his big wooden desk, sorting, completing, and revising poems and fragments of prose sketches that he had been accumulating for years on small slips of paper. Gradually these bits and pieces shaped themselves into three collections of poetry.

John Marr and Other Sailors was a set of poems and sketches dealing with seamen and the sea. They were partly inspired by Melville's visits to his brother Thomas, who had left active naval service to take charge of the Snug Harbor, a sailors' retirement home on Staten Island, and partly by Melville's increasing tendency to think about his own past. As his biographer Leon Howard says, "He was more inclined to look astern than ahead, and he seems often, when he saw an old sailor, to have asked himself what had happened to the friends of his youth, or to have let his mind dwell on other mysteries of his seafaring years."[2] Melville completed his work on *John Marr* in 1888. Only twenty-five copies of the book were printed, at Melville's expense, as gifts to friends and family members.

Another collection of forty-two poems came together under the title *Timoleon*. These poems were Melville's final reflections on his own life as well as on art and literature, which he had studied diligently for many years. They have a tone of patient wisdom, of a man in the autumn of his years who views his experiences in the long context of history and culture, not with the hot-blooded immediacy of youth. The collection was published in 1891; it was the last book to appear in Melville's lifetime.

He had planned a third collection of poems, called *Weeds and Wildings*, as a gift to Elizabeth. Many of these poems used the symbolism of flowers—which Elizabeth had always loved and Melville had grown to appreciate through his rose garden. In one poem, Melville used the sweet, sturdy flower of the red clover as a symbol of his relationship with Elizabeth, reminding her of the lucky clover he had found on their wed-

Herman Melville at the age of sixty-six, in the year of his retirement from the customs house. His books had been forgotten by all but a few staunch admirers.

ding day. Their marriage had known family troubles and money problems, and they had often been at odds over important matters such as where to live and how Melville was to make a living, yet in his final years he clearly felt devotion to his wife. Although the book was never printed, Elizabeth Melville certainly read the collection of poems and knew of her husband's plan to publish them.

One other writing project absorbed Melville between 1888 and 1891. As he cast his memory over the many episodes and tales of his years at sea, one incident kept coming to mind: the mutiny aboard the *Somers*, when his cousin Guert Gansevoort had ordered three men hanged. The *Somers* affair had happened decades earlier, but it occasionally surfaced in newspapers and magazines because one of the hanged men had been the son of a prominent public figure. Articles about the *Somers* case appeared in 1888 and 1889, and these may have turned Melville's thoughts toward that old mystery. As his imagination took hold, Melville focused not on the socially prominent victim but on one of the common seamen who also was hanged. Melville turned the story over and over in his mind, until he saw the basic question at its heart: What should be done if a man is guilty under the law but morally innocent? He tried to answer that question in *Billy Budd*, his last work.

Melville tinkered with *Billy Budd* until the very end of his life. It seems to have started as a brief sketch, then grown into a story, and then into a short novel. Perhaps Melville even planned to revise and expand it beyond the form in which we know it today. As it stands, *Billy Budd* is a fictional treatment of the *Somers* mutiny. It occurs on a British rather than an American ship, and it is concerned not just with the incident aboard the *Somers* but also with the issues of naval discipline, wartime law, and officers' powers and responsibilities over crewmen that had bothered Melville during his naval service on the *United States*.

The story begins when Billy, a young, handsome, lovable sailor, is taken off a merchant ship called the *Rights of Man* to serve on a warship called the *Indomitable*. Significantly, he says farewell to the *Rights of Man* and then innocently enters a military world in which he has no individual rights. He unwittingly makes an enemy in Claggart, the scheming, malicious master-at-arms, who despises Billy because the young sailor possesses virtues he lacks, such as honesty and friendliness. Taking advantage of his position, Claggart torments and bedevils Billy. Finally Claggart falsely accuses Billy of taking part in a conspiracy to mutiny. Billy suffers from a stutter that sometimes makes it hard for him to communicate, and now, faced with Claggart's unjust accusation, he cannot speak at all. His feeling of outrage forces him to express himself in the only way he can. He strikes Claggart—and the master-at-arms dies.

Naval law requires that Billy be court-martialed for murdering an officer. Although the captain and other court-martial officials are sympathetic to Billy, knowing that he had no intention of murdering Claggart, they must try him for his act, not for his intentions. As one officer points out, even though Claggart was evil and Billy is good, they cannot let Billy go unpunished, for such an example might encourage other sailors to attack their officers. The law is intended to preserve the order of the shipboard world. Therefore, for the good of that floating society, it must be enforced. Reluctantly, Captain Vere, who is fond of Billy, orders the young man hanged from the mast.

Just as Claggart is a symbol of all that is evil and brutal in humanity, Billy is a figure of youthful innocence and simplicity, of all that is good and uncomplicated in human nature. At several points in the story, he is compared with Adam, the biblical father of all mankind, and with Christ, the divine figure who was sacrificed under human law. But many critics feel that Captain Vere, a mature and thoughtful man who is burdened with cares and complexities, is the real hero of *Billy Budd*. Vere is torn between the demands of his head and those of his heart, between intellect and sympathy. He fol-

lows the law out of cruel necessity, knowing that he will have
to live with the consequences. And Vere is haunted by the
incident, much as Guert Gansevoort was. Vere's dying words
are: "Billy Budd, Billy Budd." Vere is a tragic father figure
who is unable to save the young man who seems like a son to
him—perhaps a reflection of Melville's own grief over the loss
of his sons.

As in *Moby-Dick*, Melville uses the ship full of sailors as a
symbol for the world full of people. In *Billy Budd*, he takes the
view that people must function within a social structure—the
individual is part of the whole. Laws are imperfect, just as
people are, and evil exists in the world as surely as good does,
but laws are necessary if people are to exist together. We may
strive to make our laws more just, but we cannot abandon law
altogether, for as imperfect beings we need rules of conduct to
guide us through life. However, we must never lose sight of
the fact that laws punish as well as protect and that there is a
moral price to be paid for every act of enforcement.

Many critics see *Billy Budd* as Melville's last word on his
lifelong search for meaning in what he calls "this incompre-
hensible world." It reflects a deep, tolerant appreciation of life
as flawed, sometimes tragic, never fully understandable, and
full of hard choices. Like Captain Vere, we must make the
best of it.

Today *Billy Budd* ranks with Melville's masterpieces:
Moby-Dick, *Benito Cereno*, "Bartleby the Scrivener," and perhaps *Omoo* or *White-Jacket*. Yet Melville's last novel was
unknown during his lifetime; it is not even clear whether
anyone knew that he was writing it. He became ill in mid-
1891, and a doctor diagnosed his condition as heart disease.
He died on September 28 of that year at the age of seventy-
two and was buried in Woodlawn Cemetery in the Bronx, a

borough of New York City. A rough-faced stone decorated with a carved scroll and quill pen mark the gravesite.

By the time of his death, Melville had been forgotten by all but a tiny handful of admirers of *Typee, Omoo, Moby-Dick, Redburn,* or *White-Jacket*—his only books that remained in print for long. He was better known in England than in the United States, and even among English readers he was known only to a few fans of sea stories. When *The New York Times* printed his obituary, it called him "Henry Melville." The *New York Tribune* reported that *Typee* was "his best book." The *Press* said that he had fallen into "a literary decline," adding, "Probably, if the truth were known, even his own generation has long thought him dead, so quiet have been the later years of his life."

Melville's death called forth tributes from a few fellow writers. W. Clark Russell, a British writer of sea stories who had corresponded with Melville, dedicated a book to him and said that his books "top the list of sea literature in the English tongue." *Typee, Omoo,* and *Moby-Dick* went back into print and enjoyed a brief, mild flurry of interest. This modest Melville revival helped establish Melville as the literary discoverer of the South Seas. His Pacific tales may have been one of the reasons that French painter Paul Gauguin sought inspiration and unspoiled beauty in Tahiti and the Marquesas Islands; Gauguin left France in the year of Melville's death and remained in Polynesia until his own death in 1903. More direct evidence survives of Melville's influence on another writer, the Scotsman Robert Louis Stevenson, author of *Treasure Island* (1881) and *In the South Seas* (1896). Stevenson, who traveled and lived in the Pacific from 1888 until his death in 1894, wrote of his delight in following Melville's path through the South Seas. Jack London, the American writer best known for *Call of the Wild* (1903), also felt the interest in the South Seas that Melville had helped to stimulate. London traveled in the Pacific several times and wrote *The Cruise of the Snark* (1911) about his voyage in the regions Melville had described.

Certainly Melville is not single-handedly responsible for the popular image of the South Seas as an exotic, unspoiled paradise of balmy weather, beautiful people, and swaying palms against a backdrop of white sand and blue sea. That image was born in the reports of eighteenth-century French and British explorers such as Louis Antoine de Bougainville and James Cook, who opened the Pacific world to Europeans. But Melville's early novels, the most popular of all his works during the nineteenth century, helped spread that image and make it popular. Their influence can be traced all the way to the much-loved twentieth-century musical *South Pacific*, based on stories by American writer James Michener, who acknowledged his debt to Melville. Bali Hai, the fictional island in *South Pacific* that represents the South Seas at their most seductive and mysterious, is said to be based on Melville's Eimeo, or Mooréa.

The modern Melville revival began in the early 1920s, when a student of literature named Raymond Weaver approached the Melville family and was given permission to examine the papers Melville had left behind in a tin box. To everyone's surprise, in addition to letters, journals, and unpublished fragments of work, he discovered an entire unpublished novel: *Billy Budd*. It was published in 1924 and introduced a new generation of readers to Melville. Weaver also wrote the first major biography of Melville and sparked new interest in the forgotten author. Soon critics, students, and the general public were reading his novels and stories, and greeting some of them as masterworks. In 1927, American novelist William Faulkner declared that *Moby-Dick* was the book he most wished he had written. American poet Hart Crane also praised the rediscovered Melville, as did English novelist D. H. Lawrence, who lived in Tahiti for a time.

Melville's place in the history of literature has changed over the years. At the beginning of his career, he was admired as a writer of "charming travel books." His nineteenth-century readers then grew baffled or annoyed by his refusal to conform to their expectations. They rejected Melville because he departed from the conventional rules of literature. In the decade after Melville's death, the flurry of interest in the man and his writing centered around his identity as a teller of nautical tales; British critic and writer W. Clark Russell called *Moby-Dick* "the best sea story ever written."

During the 1920s, Melville appeared to some people to be a romantic, poetic figure—a tormented idealist, a wandering outcast haunted by dark thoughts. A few readers cherished a romantic image of Melville as an exile from paradise, forever in love with his lost Polynesian sweetheart, Fayaway, living out his respectable New England life in spiritual anguish and rejecting all literary conventions. This image may be appealing, but it is far from accurate. Like any thoughtful person, Melville *was* tormented at times by spiritual and intellectual questions, but the only thing that haunted him for most of his life was the need to earn money, and he welcomed respectability. His rejection of literary conventions was not an act of deliberate rebellion; in fact, he tried to imitate other, more popular, writers. His books departed from standard literary form because he simply could not limit himself to a single vision of each work, not because he *wanted* to break the rules. And he was much more a philosopher than a poet, a man of ideas rather than of passions.

In recent years, readers have focused on the power of

Melville's language, symbols, and imagination. *Moby-Dick*, in particular, has been the subject of countless critical studies and is read in many countries. The names Ahab, Ishmael, and Moby Dick have entered our vocabularies, so that even people who have never read the novel recognize references to the great white whale. He has even been immortalized in a "Rocky and Bullwinkle" cartoon, in which the flying squirrel and the moose go to sea on a ship called the "Maybe Dick."

Melville's powerful imagery has inspired filmmakers. In 1956 American director John Huston brought his film version of *Moby-Dick* to the screen. A 1962 film of *Billy Budd* remains a vivid testament to the power of Melville's story of good and evil. *Billy Budd* was also made into an opera by British composer Benjamin Britten. First performed in Britain in 1951 and in the United States in 1970, *Billy Budd* is a dramatic work that has won a loyal following among fans of modern opera.

Today, *Moby-Dick* is universally recognized as both Melville's crowning achievement and a towering classic of American literature. The very thing that bothered so many people when it was published—the fact that it broke the "rules" of writing and did so with gusto—is now seen as the source of its power. Today, writers who mix genres or who create unique voices and styles are admired. Thus *Moby-Dick* is now regarded, not as a failed sea romance or mixed-up adventure story, but as a triumph of the creative imagination, an example of how vast and all-embracing a book—or a view of the universe—can be. Along with Mark Twain's novel *Huckleberry Finn* and Walt Whitman's poetry collection *Leaves of Grass*, *Moby-Dick* is considered a candidate for the greatest American book. This fact would surely surprise and delight the writer who feared that he would go down in history as "the man who lived among the cannibals."

What makes a book a classic? It must be well crafted, it must be original, and above all it must impart a significant vision or insight not just to readers of its own time but to all readers. Why do we read Melville today? And *Moby-Dick*—what does a long book about whaling have to say to us? It is helpful to remember that although Melville's long digressions about whales and whaling may seem of little interest today, in the 1850s this material was of vital interest: Melville was writing about the source of light, which, at that time, was whale oil. It is as though a writer of the 1990s used the electrical utilities, the computer industry, or the nuclear power industry as the basis for an exploration of the meaning of life.

But the significance of *Moby-Dick* goes far beyond its apparent subject matter of whaling and the sea. It is part of a thread of thought that runs through all Melville's works, from *Typee* to *Billy Budd*. To one degree or another, Melville's characters all confront the problem of evil in the universe. They ask: How are we to come to terms with evil? What do we know to be true? How should we act? Their responses range from the eager but doomed quests of young seekers in *Typee*, *Omoo*, and *Mardi* to the titanic defiance of Ahab, the humble openness of Ishmael, the resigned withdrawal from life of Bartleby and Benito Cereno, and the balanced acceptance of Captain Vere. But it is in *Moby-Dick* that Melville achieved his richest, broadest, and most sparkling expression. Once he had departed from his original plan for the book, he gave himself free rein. He believed that he could encompass humor, irony, tragedy, philosophy, adventure, and spiritual musings within the covers of a single book, and every page reveals the sense of playfulness with which he approached the task. Beneath the nineteenth-century language is a sense of fun as well as a sense of profound seriousness. *Moby-Dick* forces us to ask questions about the universe and our place in it, and it gives us Melville's fullest response: We may never know the answers, but we must keep asking the questions, and we must love one another.

Melville himself never flinched from asking difficult questions. He explored pressing social issues—immigration in *Redburn*, for example, and slavery in *Benito Cereno*—and related these issues to the universal human condition. Beneath all his work lies a deep and steady sense of the unity of all humankind, a recognition that all people are the same, and that the superficial differences of class, nationality, and race are meaningless in the face of our common humanity.

Yet although he recognized the essential unity of all people, Melville also realized that each individual mind or soul is an unfathomable mystery. Melville sought to probe that mystery through such creations as Ahab, Pierre, Bartleby, and Captain Vere. Never content with telling only the surface of a story, Melville was determined to probe its psychological depths—another of his truly modern qualities. In other writers and thinkers he admired the ability to take risks, to plunge below the easy surface of thought. "I love all men who *dive*," he wrote to his friend Evert Duyckinck. "Any fish can swim near the surface, but it takes a great whale to go down stairs five miles or more." He went on to praise Shakespeare and the other "thought-divers, who have been going down and coming up again with blood-shot eyes since the world began."[3] Melville, who explored seas of thought no other writer had entered, surely deserves to be considered one of these great "thought-divers."

In some ways, Melville's life was sad, although not quite tragic. His childhood was shadowed by worry and grief. Later, he worked with furious energy at his writing career for more than a dozen years, refusing all attempts by his family to change his course; his household was crowded and often far from tranquil. He followed his impulse to write his own kind of book, despite financial and critical setbacks. He felt an intellectual loneliness that was only occasionally relieved by friends such as Jack Chase, Nathaniel Hawthorne, and Evert Duyckinck.

Even after the need to provide for his family, together with his mental and physical exhaustion, drove him into a more conventional career, he did not stop writing. *Moby-Dick* is the crown of his career, but it is a mark of his genius that in his final years, after a lifetime of reflection, he produced another masterpiece in *Billy Budd*. Widespread recognition of Melville's greatness, however, did not come until after his death.

In *Moby-Dick*, Melville created a metaphor that, many critics believe, can be used to describe his own life and work. Referring to a majestic bird that soars above the mountains of New York State, he wrote, "There is a Catskill eagle in some souls, that can alike dive down into the blackest gorges, and soar out of them again and become invisible in the sunny spaces. And even if he for ever flies within the gorge, that gorge is in the mountains; so that even in his lowest swoop the mountain eagle is still higher than other birds upon the plain, even though they soar."[4] Melville, who created images of pure innocence and utter evil, or the heights and the gorges of the human experience, soared far above the many lesser writers of his time who are now forgotten.

NOTES

Chapter 1. Grim Beginnings
> [1] Leon Howard, *Herman Melville: A Biography* (Berkeley and Los Angeles: University of California Press, 1951), 2.

Chapter 2. First Voyage
> [1] Herman Melville, *Redburn: His First Voyage* (Evanston and Chicago: Northwestern University Press and The Newbery Library, 1969), 115–16.
> [2] *Redburn*, 180.
> [3] *Redburn*, 181.
> [4] Howard, 26.

Chapter 3. The Restless Searcher
> [1] Howard, 37–8.

Chapter 5. Home Again
> [1] Tyrus Hillway, *Herman Melville* (New York: Twayne Publishers, 1963), 37.
> [2] Herman Melville, *White-Jacket; or; The World in a Man-of-War* (Boston: L.C. Page & Co., 1950), 139.
> [3] *White-Jacket*, 52.

Chapter 6. The South Seas Novels
> [1] Hillway, 19–20.
> [2] Herman Melville, *Mardi and a Voyage Thither* (Boston: L.C. Page & Co., 1950), 524.
> [3] *Mardi*, 527.
> [4] *Mardi*, xiii.
> [5] Howard, 134–5.

6. *Redburn*, 292.
7. *Redburn*, 292.
8. *Redburn*, 293.

Chapter 7. *White-Jacket* and a New Friend
1. Quoted in Hillway, 75.
2. *White-Jacket*, 372.
3. *White-Jacket*, 374.
4. Howard, 142.
5. Howard, 147.
6. Howard, 147.

Chapter 8. The "Whale"
1. Quoted in Hillway, 43.
2. Quoted in Howard, 158.
3. Quoted in Howard, 175–6.
4. Quoted in Howard, 176.

Chapter 9. "I have written a wicked book"
1. Herman Melville, *Moby-Dick; or, The Whale* (New York: Modern Library, 1950), 1.
2. *Moby-Dick*, 282.
3. Quoted in Hillway, 89.

Chapter 10. Melville's Crisis
1. Howard, 184.

Chapter 11. The Quiet Years
1. Howard, 239.
2. Howard, 240.
3. Howard, 256.
4. Quoted in Howard, 307.

Chapter 12. Neglect and Rediscovery
1. Eleanor Melville Metcalf, *Herman Melville: Cycle and Epicycle* (Cambridge, Mass.: Harvard University Press, 1953, reprinted 1970), 331.

[2.] Howard, 320.

[3.] Merrell R. Davis and William H. Gilman, eds., *The Letters of Herman Melville* (New Haven, Conn.: Yale University Press, 1960), 130.

[4.] *Moby-Dick*, 423.

CHRONOLOGY

1712   The sperm-whaling industry begins in the American colonies

1812   United States and Great Britain go to war

1818   Transatlantic sailing ships begin the New York–Liverpool route; crossing takes 30 days

1819   Herman Melville born August 1 in New York City

1825   Erie Canal opens

1832   Allan Melville, Herman's father, dies and leaves the family in debt

1832–37   Herman Melville works to help support his family

1835–40   Peak years of the American sperm-whaling industry

1837   Melville becomes a schoolteacher in Pittsfield, Massachusetts

1838   Family moves to Lansingburgh, New York

1839   Serves as crewman on merchant ship to Liverpool, England; teaches school in New York State

1840   Travels to Illinois

1841   Signs on as crewman on the *Acushnet*, a whaling ship from New Bedford, Massachusetts

1842   Deserts the *Acushnet* in the Marquesas Islands; lives briefly among cannibal islanders; charged with mutiny in Tahiti

1843   Joins American Navy in Hawaii

1844   Leaves Navy in Boston; returns to Lansingburgh and starts writing

1846   *Typee* published; United States and Mexico go to war

1847   *Omoo* published; Melville marries Elizabeth Shaw; they move to New York City

1849   *Mardi* and *Redburn* published; son Malcolm born; Melville visits Europe

1850   *White-Jacket* published; Melville buys farm at Pittsfield and meets author Nathaniel Hawthorne; Hawthorne's *The Scarlet Letter* published

1851   *Moby-Dick* published; son Stanwix born

1852   *Pierre* published

1853   Daughter Elizabeth born

1855   Daughter Frances born

1856   *The Piazza Tales* published; Melville tours Europe and the Middle East

1857   *The Confidence-Man* published; Melville returns to the United States

1857–60 Works as a traveling lecturer

1860   Travels aboard the *Meteor*, a clipper ship captained by his brother; Abraham Lincoln elected president

1861   Civil War breaks out

1863   Moves to New York City

1864   Lincoln reelected

1865   Civil War ends; Lincoln assassinated

1866   Appointed deputy customs inspector for New York Harbor

1867   Son Malcolm dies

1876   Poem *Clarel* published; Reconstruction ends, last Federal troops leave South

1885   Melville retires from customs job

1886   Son Stanwix dies

1891   Melville dies in New York City on September 28

1924   *Billy Budd* published

FURTHER READING

Allen, Everett S. *Children of the Light: The Rise and Fall of New Bedford Whaling and the Death of the Arctic Fleet.* East Orleans, Mass.: Parnassus, 1983.

Anderson, Charles. *Melville in the South Seas.* New York: Columbia University Press, 1939.

Arvin, Newton. *Herman Melville.* New York: William Sloane, 1950.

Bercaw, Mary Kay. *Melville's Sources.* Evanston, Ill.: Northwestern University Press, 1987.

Bill, Erastus D. *Citizen: An American Boy's Early Manhood Aboard a Sag Harbor Whale-Ship Chasing Delirium and Death Around the World.* Anchorage, Alaska: O.W. Frost, Inc., 1978.

Bloom, Harold, ed. *Herman Melville.* New York: Chelsea House, 1986.

———. *Herman Melville's Moby-Dick.* New York: Chelsea House, 1986.

Brodhead, Richard H., ed. *New Essays on Moby-Dick.* Cambridge, England: Cambridge University Press, 1986.

Busch, Briton Cooper. *"Whaling Will Never Do For Me": The American Whaleman in the Nineteenth Century.* Lexington, Ky.: The University Press of Kentucky, 1993.

Cameron, Ian. *Lost Paradise: The Exploration of the Pacific.* Topsfield, Mass.: Salem House, 1987.

Dillingham, William B. *An Artist in the Rigging: The Early Work of Herman Melville.* Athens: University of Georgia Press, 1972.

————. *Melville's Later Novels*. Athens and London: University of Georgia Press, 1986.

Duban, James. *Melville's Major Fiction*. Dekalb: Northern Illinois University Press, 1983.

Ellis, R. *Men and Whales*. New York: Knopf, 1991.

Fisher, Marvin. *Going Under: Melville's Short Fiction and the American 1850s*. Baton Rouge and London: Louisiana State University Press, 1977.

Frank, Stuart M. *Herman Melville's Picture Gallery*. Fairhaven, Mass.: Edward Lefkowicz and Kendall Whaling Museum, 1986.

Franklin, H. Bruce. *The Wake of the Gods: Melville's Mythology*. Stanford, Calif.: Stanford University Press, 1963.

Garner, Stanton. *The Civil War World of Herman Melville*. Lawrence, Kans.: University of Press of Kansas, 1993.

Hillway, Tyrus. *Herman Melville*. New York: Twayne Publishers, 1963.

Howard, Leon. *Herman Melville: A Biography*. Berkeley and Los Angeles: University of California Press, 1951.

Keyes, Charlotte E. *High on the Mainmast*. Albany, N.Y.: NCUP, Inc., 1966.

Leyda, Jay. *The Melville Log: A Documentary Life of Herman Melville, 1819–1891*. 2 volumes. New York: Gordian Press, 1969.

Miller, James E., Jr. *A Reader's Guide to Herman Melville*. New York: Noonday Press, 1962.

Morton, Harry. *The Whale's Wake*. Honolulu: University of Hawaii Press, 1982.

Mumford, Lewis. *Herman Melville: A Study of His Life and Work*. New York: Harcourt, Brace & World, 1962. Originally published in 1929.

Pullin, Faith, ed. *New Perspectives on Melville*. Kent, Ohio: Kent State University Press, 1978.

Rogin, Michael Paul. *Subversive Genealogy: The Politics and Art of Herman Melville*. New York: Knopf, 1983.

Rosenberry, Edward H. *Melville*. London: Routledge & Kegan Paul, 1979.

————. *Melville and the Comic Spirit*. Cambridge, Mass.: Harvard University Press, 1955.

Sherrill, Rowland A. *The Prophetic Melville: Experience, Transcendence, and Tragedy*. Athens: University of Georgia Press, 1979.

Stackpole, Edouard A. *The Sea-Hunters*. Philadelphia: J.B. Lippincott, 1953.

Thompson, Lawrance. *Melville's Quarrel with God*. Princeton, N.J.: Princeton University Press, 1952.

Vincent, Howard P. *The Trying-Out of Moby-Dick*. Carbondale: Southern Illinois University Press, 1949.

Wolff, Geoffrey. *Herman Melville*. New York: Viking, 1987.

Zoeller, Robert. *The Salt-Sea Mastodon: A Reading of Moby-Dick*. Berkeley and Los Angeles: University of California Press, 1973.

INDEX